How is the public interest best served? It is one thing to define the public interest... it is another to pursue the interests of the public. Given the problems associated with abstract definitions, this collection of essays explores individual approaches to acting in the public interest and examines institutional strategies for advancing the public interest.

The contributors consider the practical dimensions of promoting and protecting the public interest in diverse settings ranging from policing to planning, and national defence to resource allocation. While the main focus is executive decision-making, they critique the processes and procedures that have been used to identify the public interest in the midst of personal hopes and private desires, political priorities and commercial aspirations. Drawing on their experience and expertise, the contributors have tried to show where the public interest began as a guiding administrative principle that became an effective practical tool.

Copyright Notice

Published in 2019 by Connor Court Publishing

Connor Court Publishing Pty Ltd
PO Box 7257
Redland Bay QLD 4165
sales@connorcourt.com

www.connorcourtpublishing.com.au

Phone 0497 900 685

ISBN: 9781925826784

Cover by Chevelle Hibberd
Page layout by Graham Lindsay

Printed in Australia

BOOK 2
PUBLIC INTEREST SERIES

GETTING PRACTICAL

about the Public Interest

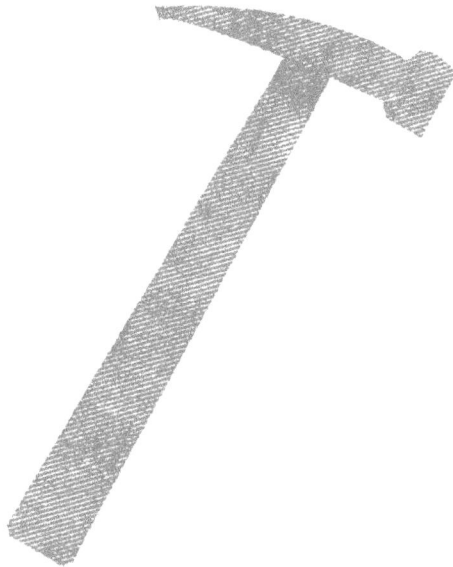

edited by **TOM FRAME**

Connor Court Publishing

Contents

Disclaimer

The views expressed by contributors are their own opinions and do not necessarily represent the position of the Commonwealth of Australia, the New South Wales and Queensland governments, the University of New South Wales, the Australian National University, the University of Queensland, La Trobe University, or any organisations with which the contributors were or are now associated. The publication of their chapter in this book does not imply any official agreement or formal concurrence with any opinion, criticism, conclusion or recommendation attributed to them.

CONTRIBUTORS

The Honourable Thomas Bathurst AC

Thomas Bathurst was appointed Chief Justice of New South Wales on 1 June 2011. Graduating with degrees in Arts and Law from the University of Sydney in 1971, he went on to practise as a solicitor in 1972. He was admitted as a barrister in 1977, specialising in corporate law and litigation and was appointed Queen's Counsel in 1987. His considerable experience in corporate law saw his appointment as a member of the Australian Government's Takeovers Panel from 2006 to 2011. Prior to his appointment to the bench, the Chief Justice served as President of both the Australian Bar Association (2008-2010) and the New South Wales Bar Association (2009-2011). The Chief Justice was also a member of the Executive Committee of the New South Wales Bar Association (2002-2011).

Andrew Blyth

Andrew Blyth is a senior member of staff at UNSW Canberra. Previously he was the former Chief Executive Officer of the Australian Capital Territory & Region Chamber of Commerce and Industry and a former chief of staff and senior adviser in the Howard Government. He holds an undergraduate degree in government and postgraduate qualifications in business and international relations. In 2012 he was awarded a Fulbright Professional Scholarship in Australia-US Alliance Studies that he used to conduct research at the University of Texas at Austin into off-grid energy solutions. He is a contributor to *The Long Road: Australia's train, advise and assist missions* (UNSW Press, Sydney, 2017); *The Ascent to Power, 1996: The Howard Government, Volume I* (UNSW Press, Sydney, 2017), *Back from the Brink, 1997-2001: The Howard Government, Volume II* (UNSW Press, Sydney, 2018); and, *Trials and Transformations, 2001-2004: The Howard Government, Volume III* (UNSW Press, Sydney, 2019). He is currently researching the role and effectiveness of think tanks in the development of public policy through a professional doctorate at UNSW Canberra. he has been admitted as a graduate of the Australian Institute of Company Directors.

Dr Wendy Craik AM

Wendy Craik is presently chair of the Climate Change Authority and the National Steering Committee for the Eradication of Red Imported Fire Ants and on the Boards of the Reserve Bank and Australian Farm Institute. Former positions include Commissioner with the Productivity Commission, Chief Executive of the Murray-Darling Basin Commission (MDBC), President and Member of the National Competition Council (NCC), Chair of the Australian Fisheries Management Authority (AFMA), Executive Director of the National Farmers Federation (NFF) and Executive Officer of the Great Barrier Reef Marine Park Authority (GBRMPA). Wendy was awarded the Member of the Order of Australia (AM) in 2007 for service to the natural resource sector of the economy, particularly in the areas of fisheries, marine ecology and management of water reform, and for contributions to policies affecting rural and regional Australia.

Professor Clinton Fernandes

Clinton Fernandes is an Australian academic and former Australian Army officer. He is the author of *Island Off The Coast of Asia: Instruments of Statecraft in Australian Foreign Policy* (Monash University Publishing, 2018). He teaches at UNSW Canberra. His principal research interest is the 'national interest' in Australia's external relations. He holds dual appointments at the UNSW's School of Humanities and Social Sciences and the Australian Centre for Cyber Security. He has appeared before the Federal Court of Australia and the Administrative Appeals Tribunal in cases relating to the declassification of sensitive national security and diplomatic records.

Professor Tom Frame AM

Tom Frame joined the RAN College in 1979 and served in the Navy for 15 years. He was the Anglican Bishop to the Australian Defence Force from 2001-2007 and then Director of St Mark's National Theological Centre from 2007 to 2014. He served as the Director of the Australian Centre for the Study of Armed Conflict and Society (ACSACS) at UNSW Canberra from 2014 before being appointed founding Director of the UNSW Canberra Public Leadership Research Group in 2017. He is the author or editor of more 45 books including *Living by the Sword: the Ethics of Armed Intervention*; *Moral Injury: Unseen Wounds in an Age of Barbarism*; and *Widening Minds: UNSW and the Education of Australia's Defence Leaders*.

Emeritus Professor Geoff Gallop AC

After an academic career in Australia and Britain, Geoff Gallop was a member of the Western Australian Legislative Assembly from 1986 to 2006. He was a minister in the Lawrence Labor Government from 1990 to 1993, Leader of the Opposition from 1996 to 2001 and, from 2001 to 2006, Premier of Western Australia. After retiring from politics, he became Professor and Director of

Sydney University's Graduate School of Government, a position he held until 2015. Geoff currently chairs the Research Committee of the New Democracy Foundation and is a member of the Global Commission on Drug Policy.

Associate Professor Jane Johnston

Jane Johnston is an Associate Professor in the School of Communication and Arts at the University of Queensland. Her research extends across critical public relations, communication and justice, and media diversity and change. She has published widely about the interface between courts and the media, most recently examining how social media has affected communication practice. Her most recent research investigates critical intersections in public relations, with publications including *Public Relations and the Public Interest* (2016) and a chapter in *Critical Perspectives in Public Relations* (2016). She is the author and co-editor of two successful public relations books which have both been published in multiple editions: *Public Relations: Theory and Practice* (co-edited first with Clara Zawawi, then Mark Sheehan); and *Media Relations: Issues and Strategies*. She sits on several journal editorial boards and is a regular contributor to the news media.

Simon Joyce

Simon Joyce is a Director with the National Disability Insurance Agency (NDIA), and has worked in the Health, Social Services and Defence portfolios in a number of roles with a focus on service delivery reform, and reform implementation. He has an undergraduate degree in Mechanical Engineering, and a postgraduate degree in Arts specialising in Strategy and Management, both from UNSW. He is currently undertaking a doctorate with UNSW Canberra and is undertaking research on leadership frameworks for senior public service officials delivering reform for government.

Professor Patrick Keyzer

Patrick Keyzer holds a Research Chair in Law and Public Policy. He is interested in how law and public policy advance human rights and manage risks. His main work on the concept of the public interest, his 2010 book *Open Constitutional Courts*, explored how Attorneys-General and Solicitors-General define the public interest when they make decisions to participate in constitutional litigation. Recent work has included a consultancy for the Law Council of Australia on family violence, working with the First Peoples Disability Network to help prepare a major submission to a Senate Inquiry on Psychiatric Detention, and co-writing a history of disability services in New South Wales. He is also part of a team of researchers exploring the ethics of using social media to recruit research participants.

Assistant Commissioner Clem O'Regan APM

Clem O'Regan is a career police officer with over 38 years of service with the Queensland Police Service. He has been the Assistant Commissioner Northern Region from 2008 to 2014, Ethical Standards Command between 2014 and 2018, and took on leadership of the Central Region in July 2018. His police career includes experience as a detective and police prosecutor, as well as in education and policy development. He holds post graduate qualifications in education and public administration and undergraduate qualifications in accounting and human resources. He has commenced doctoral studies in public leadership at UNSW. He was awarded the Australian Police Medal in 2003 for his leadership of educational reforms in the Queensland Police Service.

Lieutenant Colonel Chip Saint CSC

Chip Saint is the Chief of Staff of the Army Aviation Training Centre. He has served in the Australian Army since 1984 and graduated from the Royal Military College, Duntroon, as an Intelligence officer in June 1992. He has served in a wide variety of roles including as an exchange officer to the United States National Security Agency and as the Defence Intelligence Liaison Officer to the United States Defense Intelligence Agency. Chip has undertaken deployments to Bougainville, East Timor, Afghanistan and Iraq. He is a graduate of the Australian Defence Force School of Languages, Australian Command and Staff College and the Australian Institute of Company Directors. He holds a Master of War Studies from UNSW and is a doctoral candidate at the Public Leadership Research Group at UNSW where he is researching Defence leadership of the blended workforce.

Professor Peter Shergold AC

Peter Shergold has been the Chancellor of Western Sydney University since 2011. He taught economic history at UNSW from 1972 to 1988 before joining the Australian Public Service for 20 years. He served as Secretary of a number of Commonwealth Departments including Prime Minister and Cabinet. For the last decade he has been chair or director of a wide range of private and community sector boards. He has also stayed active in public life. He is the New South Wales Coordinator General of Refugee Resettlement, the National President of the Institute of Public Administration Australia and chairs the Forum on Western Sydney Airport. He is a Fellow of the Academy of Social Sciences' in Australia (ASSA).

Professor John Uhr

John Uhr is Professor of Political Science at the Australian National University (ANU). Awarded an international Commonwealth Scholarship, John completed a Masters degree and doctorate in political science at the University of Toronto, Canada. He was later awarded a Harkness Fellowship and spent two years in Washington, DC, at the Brookings Institution studying policy and public administration. He has worked in the Australian Parliament as a Senate committee secretary and has taught political theory and Australian politics at the ANU since 1990. He has directed the ANU Parliamentary Studies Centre and, more recently, the Centre for the Study of Australian Politics. His publications include the recent book *Performing Political Theory* (2018) and, before that, *Prudential Public Leadership* (2015). Among his co-authored books are *Leadership Performance and Rhetoric* (2017) and several co-edited books, including *Eureka: Australia's Greatest Story* (2015), *Studies in Australian Political Rhetoric* (2014), *How Power Changes Hands* (2011), *Public Leadership* (2008). Earlier books include *Deliberative Democracy in Australia* (1998) and *Terms of Trust: arguments over ethics in Australian government* (2005).

Chris Wheeler PSM

Chris Wheeler was a Deputy Ombudsman in New South Wales from 1994 to 2019 and is now a private consultant. He has over 30 years' experience in complaint handling and investigations, as well as extensive experience in management and public administration. Chris had responsibility for the public administration area of the Ombudsman's office, including public interest disclosure. He also had responsibility for major research projects (including the management of Unreasonable Complainant Conduct), and the development of guidance materials to assist public sector agencies and officials to achieve and maintain good practice in relation to complaint handling, public administration and conduct generally.

PREFACE

This collection of essays is based on presentations to a symposium held at UNSW Sydney in April 2019 and follows *Who Defines the Public Interest?*, a publication which followed a similar event in 2018. As with the first volume and symposium, the co-sponsors were the UNSW Canberra Public Leadership Research Group and the Office of the New South Wales Ombudsman.

The collaboration between the University and the Ombudsman arose from a common commitment to a wider appreciation of the public interest as a philosophical concept, a measure of political consensus and a test of personal conduct. The University offers two educational programs – the Master of Public Leadership and Policy (MPLP) and the Doctorate in Public Leadership (DPL). These programs focus on the public interest as the cause and consequence of effective public leadership. The Ombudsman is obliged by legislation and committed as an institutional discipline to apply a public interest test to the policies and decisions of parliamentarians, public servants and those in receipt of public monies. We both recognised the semantic difficulties and the practical problems associated with a term that was frequently used but poorly understood. In working together, the University could gain some excellent case studies from the Ombudsman's practical experience and the Ombudsman would benefit from the University's extensive scholarly research. Some form of collaboration seemed timely because the 'public interest' was being increasingly cited by policymakers and administrators to justify and explain their thoughts and actions.

Defining the 'public interest' as a concept and determining where the 'public interest' might reside or how it might be advanced is a matter for every citizen in a democracy. 'Public interest' discussions are not the preserve of politicians and pundits, jurists and journalists, administrators and academics. Everyone who breathes air, drinks water, drives cars and pays taxes – therefore, all human beings – have a stake in these discussions because they have a direct and sometimes profound effect on individual quality of life and the character of most social interactions. It is mistaken to think that the legislative, executive and judicial arms of government will always transcend the temptation to serve their own interests and act in the 'public interest'. Self-preservation is a powerful force in individual human nature. We should not presume that the members of groups can and will overcome the individual tendency to place one's own and known interests ahead of unknown others whose wants and needs may not seem so obvious or so pressing.

For instance, stable government has a greater chance of being effective and efficient because confidence in what lies ahead is more likely to encourage human and material investment. But political parties often confuse longevity for stability. Politicians assert that perpetuating their rule is good for the country and, therefore, good for the citizenry. Because change is associated with turbulence, reducing confidence in the future, leading to contraction in investment, followed by economic and social stagnation, they will justify their attempts to retain power in 'public interest' terms. Whatever increases the continuity of public administration becomes, therefore, attractive to politicians unable to question, let alone even doubt, that their policies and decisions might not serve the 'public interest'. Maintaining a firm hold on parliamentary and governmental power when it is motivated predominantly by self-preservation can lead to public authority being exploited for the satisfaction of private ambitions. In this case, a politician occupies public office essentially to satisfy individual ambitions and fulfil ideological objectives.

Similarly, public servants and judicial officers are liable to paternalism and prejudice. They, too, can put personal and professional interests ahead of what best serves the entire community. Indeed, representative vocational groups ranging from medical practitioners to university academics can be more strident in asserting their collective self-interest than individual doctors and scholars acting independently. A group promoting its self-interest is no less concerning than individuals doing the same thing if whatever they are pursuing subverts the public interest. The promotion of collective self-interest usually looks less selfish than individuals pursing their own interests although the public interest could suffer greater damage in the longer term by concerted efforts.

We seldom need help to identify our self-interest; we need help to collaborate in determining the things that will advance community living and enhance social harmony. Discussing, and often debating, the context and the character of the 'public interest' is an exercise of politics. These essays, although not political tracts, call for a new kind of politics. The authors want the discussion and the debate to be better informed, not just about the relative merits of any policy or decision, but of the means by which we can clarify the public (or publics) to be served and the interests to be advanced. The 'public interest' will always have a political dimension; it need not be distorted by partisan influences as the authors have shown.

In contrast to a single author volume, an edited collection requires the cooperation of a community of people. I am grateful for the goodwill of the contributors who submitted their draft chapters on time and graciously accepted most of my suggested changes to their text. Although my name appears on the front cover of this book I hope they all feel a sense of ownership of the whole volume. I also appreciate the assistance of my UNSW colleagues Andrew Blyth, Annette Carter and Trish Burgess for administering and conducting the symposium, the UNSW Canberra Creative Media Unit for producing the symposium booklets and recording the proceedings, the New South Wales Ombudsman, Michael Barnes, and his staff, especially Chris Wheeler and Tom Millett, for their support and solidarity, and Graham Lindsay and the publisher, Anthony Capello at Connor Court, for their experience and expertise in typesetting the manuscript and designing the book.

Tom Frame
Public Leadership Research Group
UNSW Canberra
December 2019

INTRODUCTION

Tom Frame

T hose who speak about the public interest in Australia often exude a sense of complete confidence that they know precisely where it resides and the things of which it consists. In 2019, the most frequent invocation of the public interest, and where it purportedly faced the greatest threat, followed the execution of search warrants by the Australian Federal Police (AFP) after classified information on military operations in the Middle East was leaked to the media. The ensuing protests from news directors and laments from government ministers prompted a spirited debate that has focussed on the need to balance the principles of press freedom with the demands of national security. Finding the balance is said to be in the *public interest*.

There have been arguments from politicians and journalists about the relative and absolute importance to be accorded the considerations to be weighed in deciding where the balance ought to be located. It was not simply a matter of press freedom or national security – one or the other. Journalists and politicians agreed that press freedom and national security were vital. The disagreement was over conflicting priorities and contested ideals: which of the many relevant considerations were more compelling or deserving of priority and why? As the debate continued, deep disagreement was also apparent on whether politicians could be trusted to decide where the public interest might lie? Should those in public office be the sole arbiters of what the electorate was entitled to know about the activities of its representatives and those who served them? Security and secrecy are very different things.

Media people believed the balance had shifted too far in the direction of national security with matters potentially embarrassing to the government being improperly hidden from journalists and effectively shielded from public examination. Did the public have a 'right to know' information that

1

was being improperly withheld on the grounds of national security when nothing imperilling the survival of the country was apparent? Was the deliberate over-classification of official documents – an alternative to refusing public access to information – deliberately subverting the public interest? These questions were not raised to provoke an academic debate or to prompt a political campaign. The angst was not coming from radical groups like the Socialist Alliance or activist organisations such as Getup! but from the mainstream. During a televised conversation hosted by the National Press Club on 26 June 2019, senior executives from News Corp, Channel Nine and the Australian Broadcasting Corporation complained that the free flow of information which was vital to the health of a liberal democracy was being impeded. In addition to the government's reliance on the over-classification of sensitive material under the guise of national security to diminish proper scrutiny of public administration, its pursuit of journalists and news organisations constituted a direct attack on press freedom and the public's 'right to know'. Specifically, the questionable withholding of information by the government was being used to prevent adverse publicity for the Australian Defence Force, whose members were being investigated for alleged war crimes in Afghanistan. Further, it was lamented, the nation's security agencies may have accessed the personal information of private citizens without due regard to confidentiality or privacy safeguards. The balance, they claimed, needed to shift towards the presumption of press freedom and open access to information unless and until the need for material to be withheld was clear and compelling. The alternative, those representing news organisations warned, was a rising culture of secrecy within which government could and would become tyrannous. In the view of journalists, elected and appointed officials could not be trusted to keep themselves accountable to the people. Hence, the existence of leaked information and the duty of the press to report it.

In reply, the Government contended that the information supplied by unknown public officials to the ABC and News Corp was effectively stolen because it belonged to the government and not its employees who were, in any event, legally bound to observe and honour the classified nature of the material they were handling. The information was transmitted illegally to journalists who were without any legal authority to receive it. They were essentially receiving stolen property while knowing such property to be stolen. The journalists committed a criminal offence when they received the material and another offence when they reported it. The two departments involved in the leaks, Defence and Home Affairs, could reasonably argue that those who leaked the information may not have been privy to its national security significance nor conscious of the consequences flowing from its disclosure to unauthorised persons.

When public officials are worried about the mishandling of information, they can avail themselves of formal Public Interest disclosure regimes which make it possible for their concerns to be considered formally without preju-dicing their future employment or career prospects. If a public official is still not satisfied, any concern can be referred to the Commonwealth Ombudsman for further consideration. To prevent the politicisation of national security, an additional layer of oversight is provided by the Inspector-General of Intelligence and Security (presently Margaret Stone, formerly a justice of the Federal Court of Australia) and by the Independent National Security Legislation Monitor (presently Dr James Renwick SC). These measures have been implemented to ensure that the handling of sensitive material is consistent with the standards expected of a democratically elected govern-ment and to prevent the unauthorised disclosure of classified information by departments, agencies and officials who might disagree politically with a government decision or policy.

The balance between press freedom and national security remains a hotly contested area of public administration and popular culture throughout the Western world with organisations such as Wikileaks committed to publish-ing leaked documents from around the world in the interests of truth and accountability. The existence of competing positions on press freedom is indicative of the complexity of defining the public interest in an open society like Australia. There will inevitably be deep differences of opinion. Politicians and officials will tend to emphasise the need for security to avoid giving a potential adversary any advantage; journalists and academics tend to empha-sise the need for freely accessible information on all areas of government activity to expose misconduct and reveal mismanagement of the nation's affairs. Unlike in the United Kingdom where the public interest is legally 'what the government of the day says it is' in relation to national security (a legacy of the 1985 trial of Ministry of Defence official Clive Ponting after he disclosed confidential information to an opposition parliamentarian about the sinking of the Argentinian battleship *General Belgrano* during the Falklands War), there has been more nuanced debate in Australia.[1] Successive governments have different attitudes towards access to public records where release of official information is demonstrably in the public interest. Labor governments have not been more consistently in favour of broader access than Liberal ones. The record of the two major parties is mixed, depending on their leaders and the circumstances.

This discussion is a near permanent feature in Australian public life with claims and counterclaims made about government secrets and official confidentiality, the government's need to protect sensitive information and the public's right to know what is being done in its name and with the use of its money. The most notable thing about the discussion for someone who can see merit on both sides is the ease with which the participants have persuaded themselves that they know why a particular policy serves the public and are satisfied that they know how a particular decision advances its interests. The public interest is always invoked with clarity and without any sense that such invocations might, and perhaps should, be contested. The press freedom versus national security debate gives an impartial observer the impression that both sides have come to believe that anyone resisting or rejecting their declarations of the public interest are either mistaken or malignant rather than concluding that depictions of the public interest offered by parliamentarians or the press might be unconvincing or that fair-minded people might simply have another view. After all, any account of interests will include values and preferences, and these are never uniform across a society. Interests sometimes diverge.

Curiously, those who speak of the public interest rarely explain what they mean by the public interest nor defend, let alone explain, their authority to define it. Government officials are portrayed as agents of the state and captives of the ruling political party; journalists are accused of wanting a controversial story for commercial ends and presume to know what interests their viewers or concerns their readers. The easy presumption of being on the 'right side of history' coupled with a lack of trust and an absence of respect among rival claimants to the public interest has prevented much progress being made in resolving real and potential disagreements over what constitutes the public interest. A refusal to be more candid about assertions of the public interest – how it can be known and where it might reside – has led to many unproductive discussions in which positions rather than principles are allowed centre stage. If there were clearer consensus on what is meant by the public interest and there were more consistency on how it is constituted, there may be a greater willingness to engage in compromise and a deeper readiness to forego narrow self-interest and to make sacrifices.

Why is UNSW interested in this discussion and what contribution can it make? One of the roles performed by scholars is to ask questions of policies and to critique decisions in terms of their consequences – intended and unintended. This role is sometimes resisted by public leaders who are frustrated with scholarly interest in the meaning of words and the construction of concepts. Scholars are chided for playing word games or being obsessed with mere semantics. This could be true, especially if scholars were trying to twist the meaning of words in order to make arguments they are constrained from pursuing as neutral participants in political discussion. Like every other professional group, scholars are also capable of promoting a personal agenda under the banner of informed debate.

Nevertheless, words are the principal means by which human beings communicate meaning and if leaders do nothing else, they engage in communication with those subject to their leadership. It may be ineffective and inefficient communication but it is often the essence of their leadership for better or for worse. Words give expression to attitudes while concepts – which are familiar clusters of words used to convey a bundle of connected ideas – are used to interpret actions. There is an important distinction between focusing on theory and overlooking practice and trying to establish the best words to use in any given situation and making judgements about the words that are used to describe a specific circumstance. A descriptive theory is only as good as the explanatory power it offers to those who use it and a prescriptive theory is only as relevant as the tangible outcomes produced by its implementation. Whereas an examination of words and concepts not only assists in making judgements about cogency and consistency, it has the potential to uncover everything from unintended bias to ideological intent.

In his well-known essay 'Politics and the English Language' first published in April 1946, George Orwell argued that 'political language' – and any language that is concerned with the public interest is invariably political

– is 'designed to make lies sound truthful and murder respectable, and to give an appearance of solidity to pure wind'.[2] He contended that in political settings the language being used was vague or even meaningless to obscure truth or hide intentions. Orwell not only attacked the use of euphemisms to conceal unpalatable truths, he condemned insincerity (an early form of virtue signalling) and sloppy thought deliberately obscured by empty jargon and convoluted speech. That there is so much speaking and writing of this kind, it becomes a contagion. It is spread by imitation and becomes the new norm. Using language in this way prevents thinking and inhibits discussion. Orwell is concerned that simplicity and honesty have given way to verbosity and deceit. Around the same time, Orwell wrote another essay with a similar theme, 'The prevention of literature', in which he explored the close connection between language and truth.[3] He thought that bureaucratic language and a good deal of academic writing was not only poor in terms of its literary quality but predictable and propagandist, formulaic and unimaginative. The consequence was a narrowed, if not straightened use of language, a loss of confidence in the capacity of language to expose lies and a dull resignation among readers that they, rather than the writer, were deficient in being unable to decipher meaning.

These two essays have received a mixed response, especially 'Politics and the English Language'. There is a reasonable argument to be made that Orwell was far too optimistic about the connection between thought and language and truth, and that he overlooked his own preferences and prejudices in what he esteemed and decried as good prose and democratic politics. But his work has prompted close consideration of political language on the ideological Right and Left, within government bureaucracies and across the universities where scholars have identified concealed meanings and interpreted mixed messages. Politics involves the choice of certain words and their use in motivating action. Hence, the close and continuing attention to political language. Words are the principal tool of the effective leader.

There are, of course, few areas of human endeavour that have aroused more intellectual interest but produced less academic clarity than leadership. Scholars with very different experiences and expertise, such as behavioural scientists and analytical philosophers, have turned the explanatory power of their disciplines on the exercise of leadership in the search for clear and compelling definitions and to identify the essence of effective leadership. The existence of many competing accounts of leading and the proliferation of contrasting leadership theories reveals the highly complex and incredibly nuanced nature of the subject. Some writers have focussed on leaders and others on followers; some have concentrated on abiding principles and others on changing contexts. Consequently, the leadership training regimes offered by business schools are very different to the leadership education programs promoted by humanities departments. There is, however, general agreement on what constitutes a bad leader and poor leadership. If nothing else, scholars have contributed a 'don't' list for leadership even if the 'do' list is much shorter by comparison.

At UNSW Canberra, the Public Leadership Research Group (PLRG) was formed in 2017 to focus attention on the relationship between assertions of the public interest and the exercise of public leadership in Australia. Although our focus is public leadership, the public interest is the essence of our work. Once there is consensus on where the public interest might lie and of what it might consist, the work of public leadership can commence and continue with greater confidence. The study of public leadership is, therefore, predicated on examination of completing claims and rival conclusions about the public interest.

The PLRG's first published volume was suitably entitled *Who Defines the Public Interest?* There was no single answer to the question that serves as the book's title. The contributors identified a number of public interests and a series of people responsible for pursing them. The absence of a clear answer was frustrating for those in leadership positions and challenging for academics who like to generalise. If there was a consensus, and it was far from clear or compelling, government ministers are entitled to claim some authority when it comes to defining the public interest. After all, they are elected to represent the public and their interests. There is a presumption that they have knowledge of those they represent and a sense of what they need and want. Ultimately, these government ministers (and their party) will answer to the public if they fail to pursue the interests of the voters.

In many instances, responsibility for promoting or protecting the public interest has also been divested to civil servants whose responsibilities and discretions are set out in legislation (or in ministerial guidelines). They too are answerable to ministers, parliaments and, ultimately, the courts if they fail to discharge their duties in accordance with the law. The claim was also made by certain contributors that a duty to advance the public interest transcended the offices of state. Lone individuals and private organisations could, and often did, pursue what they felt was in the public interest without any hint of self-interest or personal gain. We need to be reminded that states comprising legislatures, executives and judiciaries are capable of narrowly focused self-interest. Oppressive regimes, such as those in Turkey and Syria, Vietnam and China, place their political survival above the material interests of the population. Safeguarding the state's powers and prerogatives has a higher priority than the exercise of individual rights and personal freedoms.

If, then, the duty to serve the public interest is distributed across the community, is the public interest most readily determined by context? Can we gain a clearer sense of the public interest by looking at the many practical instances in which a public interest duty has been imposed on individuals and institutions and examining what they then did and why? This is quite possibly so. Hence, the title of this book: *Getting Practical about the Public Interest*. In contrast to earlier work which has looked at philosophies, theories and concepts of the public interest, this collection of essays assesses applications of the public interest as either a test, a policy or an ideal in a range of real-world contexts.

The book is divided into three parts. The first part deals with invocations of the public interest by judicial officers in the courts, by academics in their research, by pundits in their commentaries and by civil servants in dealing with citizens. The Chief Justice of New South Wales, Thomas Bathurst, observes that the courts play an important role in defining the public interest through statutory interpretation and that judicial officers need to exercise discretion in determining what the public interest requires in any case brought before them. The boundaries of that discretion are determined by laws passed by those elected to represent the 'will of the people'. Although he refers to the public interest as an 'indefinable concept', he suggests that our understanding of the public interest might be helped by a 'reasonableness' test of the kind used by a British court in its much-cited interpretation of the *Sunday Entertainments Act 1923*. The Chief Justice foregrounds the need for objectivity when considering the public interest but also the limits of objectivity when contested values are involved.

In the second chapter, academics Jane Johnston and Patrick Keyzer summarise the results of a small poll they conducted of scholars, students and civil servants with a self-declared familiarity with the public interest to determine what they understood by the concept. They noted not only the absence of general consensus and an agreed definition but also the lack of a working definition among theorists and practitioners of public administration. They concluded that a series of definitions attracting a reasonable level of consensus could be proposed if these definitions were based on criteria and values that were both understood and shared. The key was establishing a common platform from which public interest calculations could be made and rival claims assessed. They suggest a positive and constructive basis for further consideration of an agreed base and affirmed the continuing importance of the public interest in debates on economic, social and political issues.

In the third chapter, Chris Wheeler draws on his extensive experience as a deputy state ombudsman to consider the way public complaints are handled. He believes that studying complaints offers an insight into the kinds of things that some members of the public consider to be in their interests and how the state handles contrasting views of the public interest in its treatment of 'vexatious litigants'. What is the public entitled to expect from government agencies and state-sponsored (or funded) organisations, and when are these expectations (which often take the form of demands) unreasonable? There are common threads with the first chapter: who determines what is reasonable and on what basis is such a determination made? There are appeals to fairness and justice. Do they make the public interest easier or more difficult to determine given the existence of rival accounts of fairness and competing conceptions of justice? Wheeler makes the point that endlessly debating the public interest but never coming to a determination is not, in itself, in the public interest.

Chapter four by Andrew Blyth reminds us that the phrase 'public interest' is not new and that disagreements over its place in political systems date from the early annals of recorded human history. The classical Roman notion of *civitas* – the rights of the citizen – have morphed into more recent accounts of common good and social capital before references to the 'public interest' became much more frequent in parliamentary debates and political dialogue after 1965. More recently, the 'pub test' seems to have become the latest incarnation of 'civitas' although it lacks much of its nuance. Blyth contrasts the complexity of public interest calculations with the two objectives that seem to animate the 'pub test': first, is someone telling the truth about what they have said and done (or plan to do and say), and second, does their message make sense to the average Australian drinker standing at the bar of their local hotel? If someone who claims to be pursuing the public interest cannot be believed, their lack of credibility makes it unlikely they have identified the public interest. Perhaps worse, there is a perception that claims about the public interest are more likely to be dubious if members of the public cannot understand them. These are important points to acknowledge given much political discussion happens in recreational settings.

The principal theme of part two is the importance of trust in any determination of the public interest, whether it is trust in individuals, institutions or inquiries into what course of action best meets the community's needs. As a former state premier, Geoff Gallop writes with both experience and expertise about the difficulties associated with ensuring the public believes its interests are at the forefront of decision-making. After considering trust as a principle that cannot be overlooked or neglected in the conduct of state affairs, he considers the place of negotiation and compromise in securing practical outcomes that more closely approximate with what the majority of people seek from their representatives. Because politics involves competing visions of what is best for a society and its citizens, elected officials need to be flexible while showing strength. The first is needed when considering interests; the second is needed in pursuing results. Gallop's account of the public interest makes room for both ministerial advisors and public servants within a framework of clear standards and firm accountability. The right decision in public interest terms is rarely a decision quickly made.

In chapter six, Peter Shergold, one of Australia's most distinguished public servants, begins with a counter-intuitive question: would pursuit of the public interest in Australia be adversely affected were the public service to be abolished? Are public servants really needed in the sifting and sorting of rival claims about what promotes or protects the public interest? With an exponential increase in the number of advisors employed in ministerial offices across the country at both state and federal level, has the Australian Public Service (APS) become redundant? He concludes that the APS needs to stay but he advocates changes to its institutional structures, legislative framework and workplace systems. More challenging is his call for a new mindset among public servants, one that welcomes experimentation and accepts risks. His prescriptions for cultural change concentrate on the critical role played by public servants as 'go-betweens' in the interactions between an expanding community of diverse stakeholders whose assertions of the public interest often need to be distinguished from instances of special pleading.

John Uhr's chapter very helpfully complements the previous two. He draws our attention to the place and importance of 'character' in determinations and decisions involving the public interest. Character is a function of both personality and temperament. Some politicians are more naturally disposed to deciphering the public mood and discerning the public interest. Drawing on classical and contemporary literature, he considers a number of instances in which character was both a help and a hindrance to the conduct of national affairs. The first case study is Sir Henry Parkes and involves his quest for responsible government in colonial New South Wales; the second is Sir Winston Churchill and his use of classified information to embarrass the British Government over defence preparedness; and, the third is Richard Nixon and his provocation of collective disobedience among public officials in the United States Department of Justice over racial de-segregation. Uhr's depiction of character rightly foregrounds prudence as both a personal virtue and an administrative value that is worth encouraging.

The final chapter in part two draws on personal experiences gained while pursuing a professional project. Clinton Fernandes has challenged the government's decision to deny him access to official Australian records relating to the Indonesian invasion of the former Portuguese colony of East Timor in 1975. He argued at the Administrative Appeals Tribunal that release of certain documents was in the public interest and that withholding them was contrary to the public interest. Further, he notes that the public is unable to examine the case that governments might make before the courts that release of particular official records is not in the public interest. Fernandes advocates the establishment of a public interest advocate to assist the courts in determining whether the government's arguments in such cases are justified.

He fears that refusing access to historic but potentially sensitive material is more about political convenience than concerns over national security.

Part three examines approaches taken by a range of organisations to the public interest as an operating principle. Chip Saint examines the tension between effectiveness and efficiency in the delivery of reform programs within the Department of Defence over the past 30 years, and the complexities of leading a military workforce that also includes civilians, contractors and consultants, each of whom has different expectations of the tasks they are required to perform and how their responsibilities will be discharged. He thinks the modern 'integrated' workforce is placing strains on the Army's traditional leadership models while the emerging demands imposed on uniformed commanders have yet to be addressed in formal leadership training.

In chapter 10, Clem O'Regan draws on his long experience of policing in Queensland to remind readers that the mandate of uniformed law enforcement officers is neither straightforward nor free from controversy given there are so many competing interpretations of the public interest. He notes that the 'community' served by police is largely undefined in legislation which makes it open to partisan political interference. He provides a contemporary understanding of the 'Queen's peace' which has more to do with the public's confidence in the integrity and professionalism of the police than arresting and charging more people or producing an upturn in crime clear-up rates. The foremost public interest served by police, he suggests, is highly practical: preserving community peace by restraining malevolence and ensuring material prosperity by promoting due regard for property.

In the eleventh chapter, Simon Joyce poses searching philosophical questions of program delivery within the National Disability Insurance Scheme (NDIS) established by the Gillard Government. He focuses specifically on the desire to maximise participant autonomy and choice alongside the responsibility of administrators to ensure public monies are spent wisely and well. Allowing individuals to determine the supports they seek from the NDIS in a timely and unimpeded manner might conflict with the standing requirement for competitive tendering and financial accountability in the provision of services. What should happen when an individual's assessment of what best meets his or her needs conflicts with a public servant's evaluation of where the greatest public benefit might lie? He points to effective public leadership as the means by which potential impasses can be overcome.

In chapter 12, Wendy Craik looks at the complexity of managing water allocations in the Murray-Darling Basin in the context of individual self-interest and broader community concerns. In responding to allegations of 'water theft' and favouritism, the existence of multiple objectives, consumers, jurisdictions and perspectives has made it difficult for all parties to feel confident about the integrity of processes designed to promote the public's interest in preserving a scarce natural resource and regulating its responsible use. She highlights the role that independent auditors can play in generating the kind of community confidence needed to undergird trust in the transparency and accountability processes that are nonetheless essential for an effective management regime that protects shared interests.

In the final chapter, I consider the nation's universities and whether their teaching, research and engagement activities ought to be geared more towards advancing the public interest than the scholarly interests and academic aspirations of their faculty. Most universities claim to serve their host communities and the needs of the taxpayers who provide core funding. And yet, there is not a university in Australia with founding legislation or a vision statement that mentions the public interest. In considering whether they ought to make promotion of the public interest an imperative for all staff, universities appear reluctant to intrude on the institutional autonomy and the intellectual freedom of their academics who cannot be compelled to focus on what may be deemed public interest problems or, indeed, be obliged to accept the senior leadership's account of where the public interest might lie. In an era of increasing commercialisation and corporate funding, there is growing fear that universities will only serve those who fund their activities or, in pursuit of income generated by overseas students or from targeted research supported by industry groups, incline more towards activities that generate cash than deliver a public dividend.

The postscript is the next instalment in my continuing attempt to define the public interest in conceptual terms. After showing that it embodies personal virtues that rely on existential values, I have tried to depict the public interest more as a philosophical concept with wide-ranging applications than a concrete construct that draws its meaning primarily from context. My hopes of developing what might be considered a 'portable' definition of the public interest, that is, one that has utility and can be applied in a range of settings, might eventually prove to be forlorn if the arguments are unpersuasive. If so, I will need to concede that context ultimately demarcates the public and delineates its interests, and to then conclude that cogent public interest claims cannot be understood beyond the circumstances in which such assertions are made. I am not yet ready to make such a concession. There is a good deal of conceptual consistency observable in the following chapters, leading me to believe that each of the authors is essentially referring to something very similar when they refer to the public interest.

What should readers make of this book? At the very least, these essays counsel against thinking the public interest is a unitary concept. As the contributors have shown, it has been understood and applied in achieving a number of different ends, from promoting a general approach to the conduct of public administration to requiring specific decisions from private entities. This collection should certainly prompt a range of professional groups to examine their motivations. Professionals often claim to serve the public interest when their shared imperatives might lie much nearer to the immediate aspirations of their members than the common good to be enjoyed by all. While our society relies upon the skills that are curated by professional groups, we ought to be wary of more expansive claims to altruism or selflessness. There is a perennial assumption that whatever serves the interests of a professional group will eventually serve the interests of the community at large. Such an assumption is unjustified. In Australian history a number of professions have set themselves against the population or felt themselves above the public interest, acting against majority public sentiment in withholding their labour until their demands, and these have not always been monetary, have been met. I have in mind more than routine industrial action or partisan campaigns. Professional groups can place their own collective interests above those of the public when they succumb to hubris in the form of paternalism and 'virtue signalling'.

The publication of this book highlights the need for continuing discussion given the weight our society places on the public interest to ensure certain standards of behaviour among those holding public office. It also embodies the enduring conviction that a nation is not judged by the collective wealth of individual citizens but on the common life of all its people and the quality of the public spaces they frequent. In a society hosting a popular culture that tends to promote individual achievement ahead of collective aspiration, the public interest plays an important role in ensuring that individual freedoms and liberties are not pursued to the extent that a shared vision of a better community is lost from sight. While individuals are entitled to pursue their own hopes and dreams, they will never be realised if the horizon extends only as far as personal gain and private fulfilment. Human beings are social creatures and their interactions will always have a bearing on individual contentment. We all have a stake in the public interest because we all form the public and we share many interests.

Endnotes

1   For a discussion of the significance of the Ponting trial see https://www.telegraph. co.uk/news/newstopics/mps-expenses/mps-expenses-rebuilding-politic/6231381/ MPs-expenses-whistleblower-prosecution-acquitted-Clive-Ponting-The-Observer. html.
2   A copy of the essay can be downloaded from: https://www.orwell.ru/library/essays/ politics/english/e_polit.
3   A copy of the essay can be downloaded from: https://www.orwell.ru/library/essays/ prevention/english/e_plit.

CHAPTER 1

Defining the public interest: where lawyers fear to tread?

Thomas Bathurst

A sking a judge to define any term, let alone one as protean and inde-terminate as 'the public interest', is just asking for trouble. As I am sure you all know, we judges are known for trading in ambiguity and impenetrable prose. But then, it struck me. The aim of an opening chapter is not to be definitive or conclusive, but to be so vague, subtle and plausibly erudite that the reader cannot precisely be sure what point is being made. Vague, subtle and plausibly erudite are epithets which can easily describe most judges, and so the reasoning behind inviting me to contribute became clear.

I have started in this slightly self-indulgent fashion because, beneath the self deprecation, there is more than a grain of truth. The definition of 'the public interest' has always been a topic where lawyers have feared to tread, or at the very least, a topic where they have learned to tread lightly, since it has generally been seen to sit at the boundary between 'the law' on the one hand and 'policy' on the other. The question has usually arisen when a statute confers a power on a decision-maker within the executive government to make a decision based on their assessment of what the public interest requires to be done in the circumstances of a particular case.[1]

A member of the public who seeks judicial review of such a decision faces a significant obstacle in the reluctance of the courts to be drawn into debates about whether the decision-maker came to the correct decision about what the public interest required. Courts have been consistent in stating that the phrase 'classically imports a discretionary value judgment to be made by reference to undefined factual matters, confined only "in so far as the subject matter and scope and purpose of the statutory enactments may enable ... given reasons to be [pronounced] definitely extraneous to any objects the legislature could have had in view"'.[2] Put simply, while what can be considered as part of 'the public interest' is limited to some extent by the subject matter and purpose of the relevant statute, it is otherwise within the discretion of the original decision-maker to determine.

If this is all that there was to 'the public interest', then this would be a very short chapter. I could, of course, extend it slightly by talking about other areas of law which use the concept in a slightly different sense, such as the doctrine of public interest immunity in the law of evidence,[3] the defences based on the public interest in defamation law,[4] or statutes which regulate public interest disclosures.[5] But these areas of law are narrower in their scope, and I do not think that they really shed much light on what 'the public interest' means for the purposes of a general keynote. Ultimately, a simple, black-letter perspective can only tell us so much. We need to take an approach which goes beyond mere legal doctrine if we want to understand how to define 'the public interest' and its relevance for our system of government more broadly.

This does not mean, however, that we can escape the need to grapple with the relationship between 'the public interest' and the law. To start with, our understanding of the political community which constitutes 'the public' is in itself defined by the law. The existence of this community depends upon the shared belief that we are bound by the rule of law under the Constitution of Australia and governed by the laws and institutions which it establishes. The characteristics of this community, and thus the scope and meaning of 'the public' for the purposes of defining 'the public interest', must be deduced from the nature of those laws and institutions, and not from, as unfortunately can sometimes occur, beliefs based on what can be described as, at best, short-sighted nationalism, or at worst, deplorable cultural supremacism.

Let us therefore take a small step back from the narrow and technical definitions of 'the public interest' dictated by legal doctrine, and instead look at how the concept takes its colour from the nature of our political community defined by the law. Our *Constitution* must be the starting point, but is perhaps a bit misleading. Its text and structure can give the impression that the centre of the political community remains the Queen, which no longer represents reality. For a long time, it has been accepted that, under the *Constitution*, it is 'the people' who lie at the heart of the Australian political community because it is 'the people' who elect representatives to the legislature to exercise the power to make laws to define the rights and obligations of those within the community.[6]

Since 'the people' are committed, under the *Constitution*, to abiding by the decisions on laws made by their representatives, it is these laws which we must take to be the expression of the decisions of 'the people' as a whole, and not just the whims of a majority. In this way, the law can be seen to become something more than just a means of regulating how an individual ought to behave. It becomes instead an expression of 'the public will'.[7] In slightly more poetic language, we might also say that it becomes an expression of 'the whole personality' of the community, embodying the beliefs, opinions, desires and, most importantly, the values of 'the people' who have endorsed the law through their responsible representatives.[8]

Nothing in this argument is inconsistent with overriding statutes such as the *Charter of Human Rights and Responsibilities Act* 2006 (Vic). That particular expression of will by the legislature represents a determination that courts should have regard to the rights defined in that instrument in construing the terms of other legislation unless it engages the provisions which permit the *Charter* to be overridden.[9] Merely because other legislation is, to some extent, subject to the *Charter* does not mean that it is any less an expression of the public will. It merely means that the public will must be discerned by considering the two instruments as a whole.

A public official charged with the administration of the law, whether as a judge or a member of the executive government, cannot ignore this background. If the law as a whole is regarded as an expression of the public will, then the nature of 'the public interest' must, to some extent, take its lead from that will. I cannot accept that, where that will has clearly been expressed, the public interest could be interpreted as possibly requiring something which is to the contrary. An expression of will by the public must be interpreted as a decision about what their interests require. In a country like Australia, where we have full and free participation in our elections, it would be arrogant for any public official involved in the administration of the law to presume otherwise. They may think the decision right or wrong but, once it has been made, it must be respected.

Of course, the problem with this reasoning is that an expression of will by the public through their laws is often simply not clear. Many laws confer powers with a wide discretion and little guidance on how it is to be exercised, and many others are complex and technical, requiring considerable skill and expertise to penetrate their intended meaning. In either of these circumstances, discovering what the public interest requires is no easy task. A balance has usually been struck between distinct and incommensurable interests, with a necessarily unclear outcome.[10] While it is possible to see generally what might have been intended by the law, it can be difficult to understand how it applies to the facts of a particular case. To that extent, then, the public interest has been left undefined.

Now, these kinds of difficulties will be familiar to many, whether as lawyers or those involved in public administration, as problems of statutory interpretation. It might seem to you as though, through a sleight of hand, I have mistakenly equated the process of construing the provisions of a statute with determining what the public interest requires. Far from representing a confusion of thought, this is precisely my point, and I think that it follows from what I have said earlier. If it is accepted that the laws made by the legislature are an expression of the public will and a judgment of 'the people' about what the public interest requires, then it follows that any attempt to define or understand the public interest must begin with an interpretation of the relevant laws.

This analysis could be thought somewhat unsatisfactory. The idea of 'the public interest' has a long history in philosophy, and its meaning continues to be the subject of much debate.[11] It might not seem legitimate to reduce it to a question of statutory construction. And, if we are talking about how we should act in our role as members of 'the people' electing our representatives to the legislature, or about how representatives should vote on legislation, then of course this is true. In this context, each of us must be and is free to come to our own understanding of what 'the public interest', or, to use a less legalistic term, 'the common good', requires and exercise our vote accordingly. In doing so, we may draw upon the many different interpretations of the concept of 'the public interest' or 'the common good' which have been proposed over the centuries.

Nevertheless, it is a different story altogether if we are talking about how we should act as public officials who have wide discretion to exercise powers conferred by law. Here, the starting point must always be the terms of the statute, no matter how wide or unconfined the discretion may appear at first glance. Our goal must always be to understand the scope of the power which has been vested in us by the expression of the public will through conventional principles of statutory interpretation. The scope of the power and, thus, the limits on what the public interest requires, must be discerned according to the text, context, and purpose of the relevant statutory provision.[12]

I am under no illusion that this process is capable of giving a single answer in every case. In some cases, it may well be that the necessary course of action is obvious, and there is no question about what the public has adjudged its interests to require. In other cases, the decision-maker may be left in doubt. The process of interpretation may reveal the different interests which are at stake and the considerations which are relevant, but not how they are to be weighed or balanced. It is left to the decision-maker to make a value judgment as a matter of human impression based on those interests and considerations revealed as relevant through the process of interpretation.[13] This path of reasoning leads us to the conclusion that whatever courses of action remain within this margin of appreciation fall within 'the public interest'.

To some, this might hardly seem a satisfactory conclusion. It tells us little about what a decision-maker should do when confronted with a discretionary decision. In fact, on one view, our analysis collapses down to the definition of 'the public interest' propounded by black-letter legal doctrine from which we sought to escape earlier, where there is a sharp divide between 'the law' and 'policy'. We have simply affirmed that a decision required to be made in the public interest is discretionary, to some extent limited and controlled by the requirements of statute. It does not seem that we have really learned much about how we ultimately come to make this discretionary decision. Does this mean that we are forced to start again and look elsewhere to discover the meaning of 'the public interest'?

I think not. The apparent conundrum which we have encountered arises from the rather abstract nature of the discussion so far. I have been speaking in generalities, and this means that we can sometimes miss something important. In this case, I think we have missed the fact that, no matter how wide a properly construed statutory discretion seems to be, it will always pale in comparison to the number of ways in which a discretion could be exercised in a completely arbitrary manner. By focusing on the width of the discretion which still remains after all relevant interests and considerations have been taken into account, we ignore the sheer size of the number of possible interests and considerations which have been excluded.

Seen in this light, I do not think that our conclusion is as unsatisfactory as it might at first seem. It just means that we cannot delineate the process of legal interpretation as separate from the process of identifying 'the public interest'. Instead, interpretation forms an integral part of it. A decision-maker builds the idea of 'the public interest' by a process of careful construction of the terms of the power conferred by a statute in its context, paying attention to not only what it requires to be considered, but also what it implicitly excludes from consideration. Then, the decision-maker must weigh and balance these matters and make a judgment about what it is that the public interest requires. The process of ascertaining 'the public interest' will not always result in a single answer, but is a process which, if undertaken correctly, will render a decision legitimate and insusceptible of legal challenge.

This position has the consequence that the courts do have an important, but often unrecognised, and sometimes, unwanted, role to play in defining 'the public interest'. As I hope I have made clear, the law itself is an expression of the public interest and its interpretation by courts must necessarily play a part in defining what the public interest requires. Of course, a court must usually refrain from making the value judgment which ultimately determines what decision ought to be made in a particular case unless expressly authorised to do so. But this does not mean that we can remain blind to the fact that, in their role as interpreters of what must or must not be considered in the exercise of a statutory power, the courts are involved in a process of defining 'the public interest'.

Nowhere is this more evident than in the idea that a decision can be open to challenge on the ground that it is simply 'unreasonable'. While this term does have a specialised meaning within the law, recent decisions of the High Court of Australia have possibly meant that it has a much wider scope than was perhaps previously thought. In my opinion, these developments are clear illustrations of the often covert but important role that courts can play in defining 'the public interest'. In the remainder of this chapter, I want to take a closer look at these decisions and show how they are consistent with the idea that courts play an integral part in the process of defining 'the public interest' through statutory interpretation and, in particular, how the use of the concept of 'reasonableness' could make this role much more prominent.

Before turning to the decisions of the High Court, it is useful to have some understanding of how 'unreasonableness' developed as a ground of review. To do this, we need to go back in time to the 1940s to a rather quaint dispute between the owners of a cinema, or a 'picture house', as they were then known, and the local council for the town of Wednesbury in the United Kingdom, which is now on the outskirts of Birmingham. The dispute concerned the power of the council to impose conditions on allowing a cinema to open on a Sunday under section 1(1) of the *Sunday Entertainments Act* 1932 (UK). The dispute eventually made its way to the Court of Appeal, and was resolved in the famous case of *Associated Provincial Picture Houses Ltd v Wednesbury Corporation*.[14]

The terms of the power of a local council under section 1(1) were almost as broad as could possibly be. The council for an area had the power to 'allow places in that area licensed under [the *Cinematograph Act* 1909 (UK)] to be opened and used on Sundays for the purpose of cinematograph entertainments, subject to such conditions as [the council] think fit to impose'. Prior to the passage of the *Sunday Entertainments Act* 1932 (UK), cinemas were completely prohibited from opening on Sundays by the provisions of the *Sunday Observance Act* 1780 (UK). The reforming legislation had been introduced after an opportunistic solicitor's clerk had made something of a sport of prosecuting some cinemas who dared open on a Sunday in contravention of the earlier statute and, on one occasion, she had succeeded in having a penalty of £5,000 imposed on the owners of a cinema.[15]

This context is important in understanding the nature of the power which had been conferred on councils under the *Sunday Entertainments Act* 1932 (UK). It means that it is incorrect to view this power as a regressive measure.

Rather, it represented a liberalisation of the religious values concerning Sundays which had been embedded in the law by the *Sunday Observance Act* 1780 (UK). The change allowed individual councils to determine whether they would take the, at the time, progressive step of permitting cinemas to lawfully open on Sundays, with the additional option of prescribing conditions with which cinemas had to comply if they were going to open.

After the *Sunday Entertainments Act 1932* (UK) had come into effect, the Wednesbury local council had exercised its newfound power by allowing cinemas within its area to open on Sundays, but only on the condition that '[n]o children under the age of fifteen years shall be admitted to any entertainment, whether accompanied by an adult or not'.[16] Unfortunately, it is here that the historical record begins to get a little fuzzy. It does not appear that there has been any sustained investigation into the circumstances in which the owners of the Gaumont Cinema in Wednesbury attempted to challenge this condition. Regrettably, I am unable to add much colour to the facts which appear in the reported case. Nevertheless, I think it suffices to say that the owners, as reasonable businesspeople, were probably not insensitive to the commercial opportunities presented by opening their doors on Sundays to a younger clientele hungry for the novelty of motion pictures.

The owners of the Gaumont Cinema thus sought declarations from a court that the condition was beyond the power of the council to impose because it was 'unreasonable'.[17] The primary judge found that it was not beyond the power of the council to impose that condition and dismissed the proceedings. The owners then appealed to the Court of Appeal, which unanimously affirmed the conclusion of the primary judge. The judgment of the Court was delivered by Lord Greene, the Master of the Rolls. It is important to note that His Lordship accepted that the power conferred on the council to impose conditions on Sunday openings had to be exercised 'reasonably'.[18] The real question which the Court had to consider was what it meant for the council to be required to exercise the power 'reasonably'.

Much of the subsequent confusion and debate surrounding this case has arisen because Lord Greene's judgment has been interpreted as an attempt to lay down a definitive standard for what constitutes a 'reasonable' exercise of power. Hence, we have the concept of 'Wednesbury unreasonableness', which is derived from His Lordship's comment that a decision will only be 'unreasonable' if it is a decision 'that no reasonable body could have come to'.[19] I will put this concept to one side, because later cases have pointed out that it is a mistake to see this development in isolation from earlier cases or to read the words used in the judgment as if they were a statute.[20] I entirely agree. The ground upon which his Lordship actually resolved the principal issue in the case was quite narrow and briefly expressed, and made it unnecessary to consider the precise nature of what it meant for a decision to be 'unreasonable'.

The crux of His Lordship's analysis of the case is his finding that it was 'clear that the matter dealt with by [the condition imposed by the Wednesbury council] was a matter which a reasonable authority would be justified in considering when they were making up their mind what condition should be attached to the grant of this licence'.[21] If this was accepted, it then followed, almost as a matter of logic, that the exercise of power could not be legally unreasonable. If it were otherwise, then 'the ultimate arbiter of what is and is not reasonable [would have been] the court and not the local authority', which His Lordship emphatically stated could not be correct because the decision-making function was one which the legislature had expressly entrusted to the council, and not to the courts.[22] On this basis, there could be no finding that the imposition of the condition was unreasonable.

Now, I have so far skipped over stating exactly what matter it was that Lord Greene found that the council was justified in considering in imposing the condition and, thus, which supported the finding that its decision was not unreasonable. This is not because it is unimportant, but because it is the part of the case which I think is the most interesting for our purposes. His Lordship identified the matter when he explained that '[n]obody, at this time of day, could say that the well-being and the physical and moral health of children is not a matter which a local authority, in exercising their powers, can properly have in mind when those questions are germane to what they have to consider',[23] and later in his judgment, expressly identified this as a matter to be able to taken into account as part of 'the public interest'.[24]

Lord Greene did not, however, go further to identify whether this was a conclusion of law or fact, or what legal reasoning supported it. As a result, we can only ever speculate about how this conclusion was reached. Moreover, it is quite possible that it was regarded by him as so self-evident as to not require any reflection. However, there is nothing to stop us from going further and considering how we, as outsiders to the social and legal milieu of the time, might analyse this problem. In fact, I think that, for this reason, this case is a good demonstration of how a process of statutory interpretation and legal reasoning can help us to reach the same conclusion about what 'the public interest' might require as what, to many of us, might seem perhaps a rather subjective and instinctive judgment on the part of Lord Greene.

The key lies in a deeper consideration of the subject-matter, context and purpose of the *Sunday Entertainments Act* 1932 (UK), the importance of which I have already foreshadowed. The extremely wide language of the power conferred on the Wednesbury local council under section 1(1) must take into account the fact that it represented a liberalisation of the religious values concerning Sundays embedded in the law. I think that it is plausible to say that, to the extent that observance of these religious values forms part of the 'moral health' of young children, it could be thought to be within power to impose conditions directed towards their 'moral health' in exercising the power to relax those norms. Further, it must also be remembered that the power under section 1(1) was not a general one applicable to any type of business. It was a specific power directed towards cinemas. Again, I think it is therefore plausible to say that, since going to the cinema is an inherently sedentary activity, it could be thought to be within power to impose conditions directed towards the general 'well-being' and 'physical health' of children in exercising the power to permit this activity.

This is necessarily a speculative exercise, although I think that this kind of thinking can be regarded as implicit in Lord Greene's judgment. It will always be a difficult question as to how far such considerations can be said to form part of an objective process of statutory interpretation based on text, context and purpose without also shading into the personal values and opinions of those undertaking the interpretation. However, I think that it is widely accepted that this ambiguity is part and parcel of any form of legal interpretation. The question might appear to us quite starkly when we confront a case in which the values and opinions held by the judges differ appreciably from our own, but this only serves to highlight my central point: courts play an integral part in the process of identifying what the public interest might require in a given case.

I accept, of course, that there are limits on how significant this role might be, and this case is a good example. There could be no suggestion that, since the 'well-being', 'physical health' and 'moral health' of children were relevant matters for the council to take into account, the council was no longer left with any discretion at all. It still remained for the council to consider whether it felt that these matters justified prohibiting cinemas from allowing children under the age of fifteen from attending on Sundays. Further, there could be no doubt that they were not the only relevant matters which the council could have considered. It still retained a significant discretion to decide what to do in those circumstances.

Again, I do not think it is possible to provide a schema or a rubric for ascertaining 'the public interest' in such a way that will remove this residual discretion in every case. That is a chimera. However, this does not mean that the role which courts play in interpreting statutory provisions which confer administrative discretions is somehow separate from the process of defining 'the public interest'. Sometimes, the process of interpretation will result in a fairly narrow discretion which will not normally give a decision-maker much latitude. Other times, as in the case we have just considered, there will still remain a fairly wide discretion within which the decision-maker has freedom to move. But, in both cases, by framing and defining what the decision-maker may or may not consider, the court plays a role in defining 'the public interest' from the terms of the statute.

Now, I said earlier that I was putting to one side the concept of 'Wednesbury unreasonableness', largely because it seemed to me to be peripheral to how Lord Greene dealt with the issues in the case. The notion that a decision could be invalid because it was 'so unreasonable that no reasonable authority could ever have come to it'[25] was mentioned, but not explained or considered in any detail and, on Lord Greene's view, could not have been called in aid by the owners of the Gaumont Cinema. Happily, it appears that their business was nevertheless successful despite its initial failure to increase its Sunday patronage, with the cinema continuing to operate until the 1970s. Unfortunately, the premises then entered a slow decline after being sold and becoming a bingo club, which eventually closed after a fire in 2013. However, there is still hope on the horizon: there are plans afoot to refurbish the building and revive the glory days of the Gaumont Cinema, at long last, free from its former restrictions on Sunday trading.[26]

The later history of the Gaumont Cinema somewhat resembles the history of the concept of 'Wednesbury unreasonableness' in Australian law. For many years, it existed in a kind of limbo in the High Court; occasionally referred to, and even discussed, but never applied.[27] It is only in recent years that there has been something of a revival, beginning in 2013, when the High Court handed down its decision in *Minister for Immigration and Citizenship v Li*,[28] and continuing in 2018, when it handed down *Minister for Immigration and Border Protection v SZVFW*.[29] Both decisions directly addressed the role which 'reasonableness' plays in the process of discretionary decision-making in Australian law, although they perhaps fell short of the definitive guidance for which many might have hoped.

I believe, however, that these decisions clearly have the capacity to bring about an important change in the relationship between courts and decision-makers by making the role which courts have in defining 'the public interest' more prominent. If a decision may be reviewed based on whether it is 'reasonable' or not, then this could cause courts to shift their focus away from what the terms of the relevant statutory provision objectively require and encourage them to place greater reliance on their own subjective assessment of what falls within 'the public interest'. Needless to say, this poses some significant questions about the proper place of the courts within our constitutional structure.[30]

Fortunately, for the purposes of this chapter, I think that these concerns can be set aside. I think that it is clear that the High Court was conscious of these difficulties in *Li* and *SZVFW* and was careful to explain the concept of 'reasonableness' in such a way so as to limit the extent to which courts can use it to import their own subjective judgments about what the public interest might require into their review of administrative decision-making. However, the potential remains for a wider view to be taken of what it means for a decision to be 'reasonable', as has happened or is happening in the United Kingdom and other common law jurisdictions, where it appears that it has come to include considerations of proportionality.[31]

We will still be a comfortable distance away from this position in Australia if the approach taken in *Li* and *SZVFW* is maintained. To explain that approach, it is necessary to refer to the facts and statutory context of those decisions in more detail. Both cases concerned what might be termed the 'procedural powers' of the Migration Review Tribunal and the Refugee Review Tribunal in hearing and determining applications for review of visa decisions. While this is perhaps less exciting to modern eyes than local councils imposing restrictions on Sunday trading, these decisions are a good demonstration of how the requirement that a decision be 'reasonable' increases the role of courts in defining 'the public interest'.

I will start with the decision in *Li*. A delegate of the Minister for Immigration refused Ms Li's application for a skilled visa because her skills assessment had contained information which was false, apparently through the fault of her migration agent.[32] Ms Li applied to the Migration Review Tribunal for review of the decision. For the purposes of the review, Ms Li attempted to obtain a fresh skills assessment but the process was delayed by the relevant authority.[33] Ms Li was therefore unable to provide the assessment to the Tribunal within the timeframe it had set. She requested an extension of time so that she would be able to obtain the skills assessment, without which it was not possible for her review application to succeed.[34] However, the Tribunal refused her request and dismissed her application for review.[35]

The High Court unanimously held that the decision of the Tribunal to refuse Ms Li's request for an extension of time was unreasonable and therefore invalid. While there were some differences in the approaches of the judges who heard the case, I will focus on the majority reasoning of Justices Hayne, Kiefel and Bell. Further, while their Honours' explanation of the history and legal nature of 'Wednesbury unreasonableness' is instructive,[36] I want to look more closely at how they analysed the particular circumstances of the case before them.[37] It is here that we can best see how their Honours intended the criterion of 'reasonableness' to be applied.

Their Honours started their analysis by examining the reasons given by the Tribunal for exercising its power to dismiss the review application. They viewed the decision as resting on the bases that 'Ms Li had been provided with enough opportunities to present her case' and that 'the Tribunal was not prepared to delay the matter any further'. While their Honours questioned this characterisation of the facts by the Tribunal, they stated that, even if it was accepted that the Tribunal was required to take into account 'efficiency' as a consideration in determining whether to extend the time for Ms Li, it was necessary for this object to be weighed against the objects of the provisions which required the Tribunal to afford an opportunity to the applicant to 'present evidence and arguments 'relating to the issues arising in relation to the decision under review'.[38]

Their Honours then noted some of the factual circumstances which might have been relevant for the Tribunal to take into account in determining the weight of this matter, such as the fact that the skills assessment was the only matter remaining in issue on Ms Li's visa application and that she had indicated that a new assessment had been sought and would be provided as soon as it was available. They stated that it was 'not apparent' why the Tribunal had decided to dismiss the review application, thus depriving Ms Li of the opportunity of providing a fresh skills assessment when the Tribunal knew that there was a prospect of Ms Li being able to provide a new assessment to the Tribunal in the near future.[39] Their Honours rejected the idea that the earlier false skills assessment could have been an alternative justification for taking this course.[40]

The finding that there was no reason which could explain why the Tribunal deprived Ms Li of her opportunity to provide a fresh skills assessment in the circumstances which it had before it appears to have been critical to their Honours' conclusion that Tribunal's decision was invalid. They said that '[i]n the circumstances of this case, it could not have been decided that the review should be brought to an end if all relevant and no irrelevant considerations were taken into account and regard was had to the scope and purpose of the statute'.[41] While they did not use the same language, this conclusion also bears obvious similarities to their Honours' statement earlier in the judgment that '[u]nreasonableness is a conclusion which may be applied to a decision which lacks an evident and intelligible justification'.[42]

It is instructive to note how this reasoning differs from the corresponding analysis undertaken by Lord Greene in *Wednesbury*. Once His Lordship was content to accept that the 'well-being and the physical and moral health of children' was a relevant matter for the Wednesbury local council to take into account, there was no suggestion that there was any countervailing matter which the council was required to have regard by the relevant statutory provisions. By contrast, in *Li*, the majority reasoned that the Tribunal could not behave similarly and simply rely on an appeal to some generalised idea of 'efficiency' or a notion that 'enough is enough' to justify its decision to dismiss the review application.[43] The Tribunal was also required to take into account the fact that it had a duty to provide Ms Li with an opportunity to present evidence and arguments on her application.

So far, this reasoning does not go beyond what would normally be expected of a court interpreting the terms of the statutory power which conferred a discretion on a decision-maker. It is the following step which is novel. Their Honours then went on to find that it was not possible, in the circumstances of the case, to properly take both of these matters into account and to make the decision which the Tribunal did, presumably because they found no 'evident and intelligible justification' for the decision. In this sense, the decision was 'unreasonable'.

I do not think that it can be denied that this conclusion expands the role which courts can play in defining 'the public interest'. Certain decisions which might appear open on the face of the statute can be excluded from being legitimate determinations of what the public interest requires by reason of the judgment of the court, simply because it reaches a conclusion that the reasoning of the decision-making was unjustified. But it is possible to overstate the significance of this conclusion. On one view, the reasoning of Justices Hayne, Kiefel and Bell was closely tied to their interpretation of what the relevant statutory provisions required the Tribunal to consider. The simple and confined nature of the power which the Tribunal was exercising meant that it was relatively easy to see that there was no real justification for depriving Ms Li of her opportunity to present her forthcoming fresh skills assessment to the Tribunal.

I think that the decision in *SZVFW* highlights this point quite well. Its facts are quite similar to *Li* and, although there was perhaps some greater variation in how their reasons were expressed, all members of the Court once again agreed in the result. Relevantly, for present purposes, it concerned a decision of the Refugee Review Tribunal to dismiss a review application after receiving no response to several requests it made to the applicants to provide submissions and material to support their application and to attend a hearing before the Tribunal.[44] It appeared that the applicants had also failed to respond to similar requests in relation to their primary visa application.[45] Each member of the Court found that, in these circumstances, the Tribunal was entitled to have made the decision to dismiss the review application.[46]

The relevant similarities and differences with *Li* will be readily apparent. While not all members of the Court expressed themselves in the following way, I think the significant difference lies in the presence of at least some justification for the Tribunal to make the decision which it did, so that, when viewed against the detailed requirements of the statutory scheme regulating the decision-making power of the Tribunal, there was some 'evident and intelligible justification' for its actions. Importantly, I do not think that the analysis of the judges of the Court could be construed as suggesting that the conclusion which the Tribunal reached was the only one possible in those circumstances. By contrast, it was only because the situation in *Li* was exceptional that the Court had been prepared to hold that it was not possible for the Tribunal to have reached the conclusion that it did.

It is impossible to do justice to the nuances of this area of law in a reasonably brief chapter, and I have not tried to do so. Instead, I have used it as an example of how the courts play an important role in defining 'the public interest' through statutory interpretation, and this is all the more the case since *Li* has confirmed the continued existence of 'reasonableness' as a ground of review for administrative decisions. However, it must always be remembered that this process, since it is based on the principles of statutory interpretation, is controlled by objective considerations. It does not and should not give judges a warrant to interfere with decisions based on their personal opinions and values. While the requirement that a decision be 'reasonable' may result in a narrowing of the discretion remaining with the decision-maker, it is not the place of courts to wholly subsume this discretion unless expressly authorised to do so by the legislature.

If we were to go further afield, there are other areas of law where courts are regularly required to make determinations about what the public interest requires, even if this label is not expressly used. One clear example is defining what constitutes 'unconscionable' conduct for the purposes of trade practices legislation,[47] or what constitutes a 'legitimate purpose' for the analysis required by the implied freedom of political communication.[48] There can be no doubt that the responsibility for defining what is included within these concepts and other similarly 'fuzzy' concepts falls wholly on the courts, and this necessarily involves them engaging with 'the public interest'. But, the principles which have been developed to govern the interpretation of these concepts are, in many respects, quite different from those which prevail within the administrative law context I have been discussing. I refer to these examples only to point out that the role which courts have in that context is hardly unusual or unprecedented.

In the end, public officials, whether judges or members of the executive government, will always be faced with difficult decisions about what the public interest requires. These decisions will inevitably involve the exercise of discretion. What is essential is that the exercise of this discretion is controlled within the boundaries established by law, representing the will of 'the people' acting through their elected representatives in the legislature. These boundaries themselves play an important part in defining and constructing what 'the public interest' requires, and to the extent that courts are called upon to interpret these boundaries they, too, participate in the process of determining the nature of that indefinable concept, 'the public interest'.

Endnotes

1   For the purposes of this chapter, I set to one side the so-called 'fourth branch' of government: see Chief Justice Thomas F Bathurst, 'New Tricks for Old Dogs: The Limits of Judicial Review of Integrity Bodies' (2018) 14(1) *Judicial Review* 1; *Kaldas v Barbour* [2017] NSWCA 275.

2   *O'Sullivan v Farrer* (1989) 168 CLR 210, 216 (Mason CJ, Brennan, Dawson and Gaudron JJ); *Osland v Secretary, Department of Justice [No 2]* (2010) 241 CLR 320, 329 [13] (French CJ, Gummow and Bell JJ).

3   See J D Heydon, *Cross on Evidence* (LexisNexis, 11 edition, 2017) chapter 14.

4   See for example, *Defamation Act 2005* (NSW) sections 29, 30, 31.

5   See for example, *Public Interest Disclosures Act* 1994 (NSW); *Public Interest Disclosure Act* 2013 (Cth).

6   See for example, *Bistricic v Rokov* (1976) 135 CLR 552, 566 (Murphy J); *Australian Capital Television Pty Ltd v Commonwealth* (1992) 177 CLR 106, 138 (Mason CJ).

7   Cf *Singh v Commonwealth* (2004) 222 CLR 322, 329 [5] (Gleeson CJ). See also Chief Justice James Allsop, 'The Foundations of Administrative Law' (Speech, Whitmore Lecture, 4 April 2019) pp. 2–3.

8   See Chief Justice James Allsop, 'The Law as an Expression of the Whole Personality' (Speech, Maurice Byers Lecture, 1 November 2017), quoting Sir Maurice Byers, 'From the Other Side of the Bar Table: An Advocate's View of the Judiciary', (1987) 10 *University of New South Wales Law Journal*, no. 10, 1987,pp 179, 182.

9   *Charter of Human Rights and Responsibilities Act 2006* (Vic) ss 31, 32.

10   Murray Gleeson, 'The Meaning of Legislation: Context, Purpose and Respect for Fundamental Rights', *Public Law* Review, no. 20, 2009, pp. 26, 32–3.

11   Chris Wheeler, 'The Public Interest Revisited – we know it's important but do we know what it means?', *AIAL Forum* no. 72, 2013, pp. 34–5. For further discussion on the philosophical aspects of 'the public interest' and 'the common good', see the interesting discussion in Waheed Hussain, 'The Common Good', *Stanford Encyclopedia of Philosophy* (accessed 26 February 2018) <https://plato.stanford.edu/entries/common-good/>.

12   *Alcan (NT) Alumina Pty Ltd v Commissioner of Territory Revenue (NT)* (2009) 239 CLR 27, 46– 7 [47] (Hayne, Heydon, Crennan and Kiefel JJ); *SZTAL v Minister for Immigration and Border Protection* (2017) 262 CLR 362, 368 [14] (Kiefel CJ, Nettle and Gordon JJ).

13   Chief Justice James Allsop, 'The Foundations of Administrative Law', Whitmore Lecture, 4 April 2019, p. 3.

14   *Associated Provincial Picture Houses Ltd v Wednesbury Corporation* [1948] 1 KB 223.

15   See *Orpern v Haymarket Capitol Ltd* (1931) 47 TLR 575; *Orpern v Haymarket Capitol Ltd* (1931) 145 LT 614.

16   [1948] 1 KB 223, 227.

17   [1948] 1 KB 223, 227, 224.

18   [1948] 1 KB 223, 227, 229.

19   [1948] 1 KB 223, 227, 230, 234.

20   See *Re Minister for Immigration and Multicultural Affairs; Ex parte Applicant S20/2002* [2003] HCA 30, [67]–[68] (McHugh and Gummow JJ); *Minister for Immigration and Citizenship v Li* (2013) 249 CLR 332, 362–5 [64]–[71] (Hayne, Kiefel and Bell JJ).

21   [1948] 1 KB, 223, 229–30.

22   [1948] 1 KB, 230.

23   [1948] 1 KB, p. 230.

24   [1948] 1 KB, p. 233.

25   [1948] 1 KB, p. 234.

26   For the history of the Gaumont Cinema, see 'Silver Cinema', *Cinema Treasures* (Web Page) <http://cinematreasures.org/theaters/32515>; Richard Guttridge, 'Historic Gaumont Cinema Turned Bingo Club to Be Brought Back To Life in Wednesbury', *Express & Star* (online, 17 August 2017) <https://www.expressandstar.com/news/localhubs/sandwell/wednesbury/2017/08/17/historic-gaumont-cinema-to-be-brought-back-to-life.

27   See *Minister for Immigration and Citizenship v Li* (2013) 249 CLR 332, 336 (J Gleeson SC); cf *Re Minister for Immigration and Multicultural Affairs; Ex parte Applicant S20/2002* [2003] HCA 30, [67] (McHugh and Gummow JJ).

28   (2013) 249 CLR 332.

29   [2018] HCA 30.
30   Cf *Attorney-General (NSW) v Quin* (1990) 170 CLR 1, 35–6 (Brennan J).
31   See *R (Keyu) v Secretary of State for Foreign and Commonwealth Affairs* [2016] AC 1355, 1408–9 [131]–[134] (Lord Neuberger PSC). For a detailed discussion of the United Kingdom case law, see Harry Woolf et al, *De Smith's Judicial Review,* Sweet & Maxwell, eighth edition, 2018, chapter 11.
32   (2013) 249 CLR 332, 353 [34] (Hayne, Kiefel and Bell JJ).
33   (2013) 249 CLR, 353 [35].
34   (2013) 249 CLR, 354 [37]–[38].
35   (2013) 249 CLR, 355 [40].
36   (2013) 249 CLR, 362–7 [63]–[76].
37   (2013) 249 CLR, 367–9 [77]–[85].
38   (2013) 249 CLR, 368 [80].
39   (2013) 249 CLR, 368–9 [83].
40   (2013) 249 CLR, 369 [84].
41   (2013) 249 CLR, 369 [85].
42   (2013) 249 CLR, 367 [76].
43   (2013) 249 CLR, 368 [80]–[81].
44   [2018] HCA 30, [99]–[107] (Nettle and Gordon JJ).
45   [2018] HCA 30, [100]–[101].
46   [2018] HCA 30, [14] (Kiefel CJ), [70] (Gageler J), [123] (Nettle and Gordon JJ), [140]–[141] (Edelman J).
47   See for example, *Competition and Consumer Act 2010* (Cth) sch 1 s 22; *Ipstar Australia Pty Ltd v APS Satellite Pty Ltd* [2018] NSWCA 15.
48   *Lange v Australian Broadcasting Corporation* (1997) 189 CLR 520. For the most recent discussion of how this 'legitimate purpose' is identified, see *Club v Edwards* [2019] HCA 10.

CHAPTER 2

Seeking definitional consensus

Jane Johnston and Patrick Keyzer

M ore than 60 years ago American political science scholar Frank Sorauf called the public interest 'the X factor, the imponderable and unknown, in the political equation'.[1] Sorauf saw that the public interest was so nebulous that it invited 'absorption' rather than definition.[2] A decade later another leading political scientist, E Pendleton Herring, likened the idea of the public interest within the bureaucracy to 'due process' in the judiciary, noting: 'Its abstract meaning is vague but its application has far-reaching effects'.[3] Decades later, public policy scholar Barry Bozeman called it a conundrum: 'nearly everyone is convinced that the public interest is vital in public policy and governance, but there is little agreement as to exactly what it is'.[4] The former Deputy Ombudsman of New South Wales, Chris Wheeler, agreed. He observed that 'while it is one of the most used terms in the lexicon of public administration, it is arguably the least defined and least understood'.[5]

The lack of an agreed definition of 'the public interest' has attracted continuing attention from scholars since the mid-twentieth century.[6] The lack of a working definition is both a curiosity and challenge to scholars and practitioners alike, in part due to the paradox of its lack of definition and its prevalence within the texts and discourse of deliberative democracies, civil society and political and legal discourse.[7]

Public interest regulation scholar Barry Mitnick argues that the public interest is 'elusive in content although understood in construction'.[8] But is it?

Is it understood by all, or perhaps only by those who construct it? Is it sufficient to *assume* an understanding of what is meant by the term the 'public interest' without both regularly interrogating it and attempting to move it from the realm of the abstract to something more concrete? The lack of definition is blamed for its indiscriminate use and (mis)appropriation, used as a 'get-out-of-jail-free' card because of its ambiguity and malleability.[9] Critics warn that the concept may lack substance and be 'hijacked' within political discourse for unworthy ends. Leading economist Ross Garnaut points out:

> Political leaders and parties can associate themselves with public interest objectives, or align themselves with private interest. In the latter case, they can catch a ride on others' marketing of a deceitful version of the common good.[10]

Many experts argue that the only way the meaning of the public interest can be determined is within contexts and according to specific circumstances.[11] As such, the one aspect of the concept that seems to be widely agreed is that the public interest should reflect contemporary public values, mores and expectations. As famously stated by Lord Hailsham of the United Kingdom's House of Lords in 1978: 'The categories of the public interest are not closed, and must alter from time to time whether by restriction or extension as social conditions and social legislation develop.'[12] Decades later, Justice Leveson, in his report into the *Culture, Practices and Ethics of the National Press in Britain* (2012), affirmed how the public interest should reflect the values and expectations of society. His Honour noted the need for 'wider debate on the definition of the public interest, in particular if it is to gain enhanced status as a defence in the courts.'[13]

So, while the definition of the 'public interest' remains elusive, the concept requires diligent, continuing attention – both within the academy and within political, legal and regulatory environments. Scholars and critics note that it should be reviewed on a regular basis because of its time-specific and contextual nature.[14] We took the opportunity to do just that in the research we set out below, seeking to respond to two questions that emerge from the literature discussed above:

Is the public interest capable of definition in the abstract, that is, outside of specific decision-making contexts?

Given the opportunity, will experts define the public interest by reference to a range of criteria and articulated values and, if so, what are they?

Seeking a definition of the public interest through qualitative research

We undertook our research experiment with the active involvement of a room full of experts who had gathered specifically to interrogate the concept at the 'Getting Practical about the Public Interest' symposium held at the University of New South Wales (UNSW). The purpose of our inquiry was to find a snapshot of the defining elements of the public interest in a place (Australia) and at a time (April 2019). We asked the expert audience of approximately 40 people at the symposium what they understood about the public interest seeking to identify whether our questions could be answered. We specifically avoided advancing any definition ourselves.

There is a dearth of published scholarship on the use of qualitative research techniques to generate definitions of the public interest. To the best of our knowledge the only other time a definition had been crowd sourced was when *The Guardian* newspaper in Britain made a call for a definition from members of the public, finding no real common ground from 150 responses.[15] Our study, presented in this chapter, provides arguably the first qualitative attempt in Australia to bring together a group of experts to explore both key elements and definitions of this commonly used part of public and political discourse. It enabled us to test the idea that reference to community expectations and values are essential components in determining the public interest at any given time.

Methodology

Delegates at the 'Public Interest' symposium held at UNSW Sydney on 16–17 April 2019 all had a strong interest in the public interest and together they represented a high concentration of expertise and experience in applying and examining how the concept is used in public administration, law and politics. The group comprised ombudsmen and other public administrators, lobbyists, politicians and retired politicians, lawyers and a judge and scholars (academics including graduate students) from a range of disciplines including government, law and business. Most (but not all) members of the group took part in the workshop which had been set up to gather data about what members believed to be the public interest and its constituent parts. All participant responses were provided anonymously. In the time frame given, first of approximately one hour, followed by two short feedback sessions, we did not seek to examine how the concept of the public interest is applied. Elsewhere at the symposium, presentations and panels covered applied thinking about the public interest on a range of topics, including, for example, water security, immigration and the National Disability Insurance Scheme. The many other panels and presentations explored possible common ground on the meaning of the public interest in specific contexts, as outlined in later chapters in this book. Our workshop sought only to drill down into key words and definitions to develop some clarity around the language of the public interest and what it meant to the audience. We anticipated a wide range of responses.

The workshop used a version of the qualitative participatory methodology called Nominal Group Technique (NGT) as outlined by Delbecq and VandeVen[16] and Bartunek and Murnighan[17] and more recently Totikidis[18] and Keyzer et al[19], to generate ideas from within the group, workshop them and seek some consensus in outcomes. In this case, the NGT was used to gather data on how participants viewed the language associated with the public interest. The workshop deviated from a pure version of NGT by incorporating elements of brainstorming in the process. Since NGT requires people to work solo, our process of brainstorming ideas around tables departed from the 'pure' NGT process. Brainstorming (also called group ideation) was useful in this project as it is known for group problem-solving in which a group of people use their collective intelligence to approach a creative problem.[20] Together, these two techniques provided us with a solid framework for drawing out what we needed from the group. In time, the data we elicited in the experiment can be used to produce a questionnaire with content and construct validity that we can publish to a much larger sample of people.[21] The methodology followed the five stages outlined below.

First, the workshop facilitators (the chapter authors) introduced and explained the concept of the session, including distribution of consent form, information sheet and several sheets of blank (white) paper.

Second, delegates were asked to focus on individual 'silent generation of ideas' and then write down ideas that came to mind when considering the questions:

> How do *you* define the public interest?
> What are the key words/phrases that must be included in any definition of the public interest?

During this period, delegates were requested not to consult or discuss their ideas with others.

Third, delegates were asked to share the ideas they had generated amongst others at their table. Each table was issued with a three-columned piece of (pink) paper. Different coloured sheets ensured the bundles could not be confused during the data analysis. (A third colour, green, was later introduced).

Ideas were summarised by a designated table leader into:

· column 1: key words provided and frequency of key words
· column 2: definitions that emerged from the table discussion, in light of the earlier, individually determined definitions and key words/ phrases, above
· column 3: an agreed table definition

Fourth, the ideas generated from the table on pink sheets of paper were collected and analysed. In keeping with the NGT methodology, we ranked the key words/phrases and listed the definitions following our workshop. After analysing the data, we collated and compiled a list of the most popular key words/phrases (n=12) and all the agreed table definitions (n=9) (see below).

Fifth, at the conclusion of the day, we reported back to the whole group with this full list of key words and definitions and asked delegates to rank these. This was done individually in a secret 'voting' ballot, on a new green piece of paper which was collected and analysed. The voting results were then reported back to the group at the second day of the symposium. Consistent with the NGT approach, this showed the group how their collective ideas had been ranked. We now explain our findings.

Findings and discussion

Individual definitions and key words and phrases

Individual members of the expert group offered a wide variety of definitions of the public interest which we have set out in an appendix to this paper. They also developed a list of key words and phrases. We engaged in a modest amount of data cleaning (for example, one respondent defined the public interest simply as 'the public interest' which we discarded) and aggregated the answers to produce a list. The numbers in parentheses, below, reflect the number of times that the group identified the key word or phrase as important; the slash marks divide up the different but equivalent or similar key words offered by the group. Each of the items in number 12, below, were single responses so we included them together for convenience:

1. benefit to the community as a whole/benefit to the public collectively/the greater good/the common good/bipartisan (17)

2. majority interests/representative/democratically-informed/public will/will of the people (8)

3. broader – more than sectional, larger, national, decisions (6)

4. sustainability/inter-generational/precautionary principle/triple bottom line (6)

5. law, legislation-based, legal (4)

6. minority rights (3)

7. engaged with the interested and affected/consultative (3)

8. reasonable (2)

9. transparent (2)

10. public integrity (2)

11. balanced (2)

12. actions, protected, beneficial, reviewable, beliefs, rules, actions, agreed, represent, values, equity, relevance, 'relevant' public, fairness (substantive), fairness (procedural)/due process, avoidance of conflicts, deliberation, aspirations, ambitions, honesty, informed,

defensible, articulated and advanced, defined and defended, promoted and protected, safety, wellbeing, welfare, just, exclusion of private interests, not for personal gain, publicly accountable, impartial, objective, human rights, society, having regard to relevant considerations.

We accept the coding in our study includes, by necessity, a degree of subjectivity in order to make sense of the raw data, consistent with qualitative techniques that seek rich data outcomes rather than claims to replication.[22] As Schram points out, qualitative research is used to embrace 'complexity, uncovering and challenging taken-for-granted assumptions'.[23] A number of clear trends emerged.

First, respondents placed considerable weight on the *volume* (or weight) of democratic support in any conception of the public interest (items 1 and 2, and also 6 in the list above). Second, respondents recognised that the nature of the decision itself – whether it was a *broader – more than sectional*, *larger* or *national* decision or whether it was concerned with environmental matters (which also raise issues of such magnitude) – had a bearing on how the public interest should be defined (items 3 and 4). These responses reinforce the proposition advanced by scholars who emphasise the importance of context in any definition of the public interest; so, for example, a significant number of respondents identified environmental concerns as being significant components of the definition of the public interest – but such concerns would not arise in every decision-making context. Third, respondents understood process values to be important in any definition of the public interest (items 5 and 7–11).

As noted above, NGT then contemplates that the group votes on the list that has been developed. We therefore invited people to vote for their top 12 key words/phrases from the list above, and then their top 6 from that 12. In the list below, the top 12 are listed, and then the bottom 6 of the 12 are struck through, with the information in parentheses showing how particular items from the top 12 shifted around after the second vote:

1. Benefit to the community as a whole/benefit to the public collectively/the common good (was 1st on the initial list of 12)

2. Transparent (was 11th)

3. Majority interests/public will/will of the people/democratically informed (was 2nd)

4. Law/legal/rules/legislation-based (was 6th)

5. Sustainability/inter-generational equity/precautionary principle/ triple bottom line (was 3rd)

6. Broader – more than sectional, larger, national/national interest decisions (was 4th)

7. ~~Minority rights~~

8. ~~Engaged with the interested and affected/consultative~~

9. ~~Shared values~~

10. ~~Reasonable~~

11. ~~Public integrity~~

12. ~~Balanced~~

The narrowing down and sharpening required by the voting method adopted had several clear effects. The individuals making up the whole group confirmed their support for the 'common good' and 'majority interests' definitions of the public interest (items 1 and 3). Transparency jumped to second place and was seen as more important than other process values such as reasonableness (item 2). The importance of laws was reinforced (item 4). Interestingly, what may be broadly termed 'environmental concerns' remained prominent (item 5), whereas initially, when the respondents were working solo, only six of the initial respondents in the group had identified these as matters of significance.

Based on the 'top 12', a broad definition of the public interest may be constructed as follows:

> The public interest is concerned with the common good, or majority interests, while being mindful of minority rights. The public interest requires transparency in a legal, rules-based order. The public interest is often concerned with decisions of a broader nature. The public interest requires concern for sustainability and inter-generational equity, and recognition of the need to protect the environment and maintain a triple bottom line. It is concerned with the consultative achievement

of shared values in a decision-making process that is reasonable, has integrity, and is balanced.

Table definitions

As noted already, we also requested each of the nine tables to develop a single 'table definition' of the public interest and submit these. This part of the study drew on the brainstorming methodology, outlined above. The nine definitions were then voted on. In the following section we set out the findings, listing first each table definition, followed by the raw votes (that is, the number of individual votes for each item, weighted by reference to its position on each voter's list of preferences), with the final rankings set out at the end of each item.

1. Decisions or actions for the common good of the relevant public. (213) 1st

2. The set of shared values that reasonably reflect those of the greater public, as reflected in the laws/rules of the group. (187) 2nd

3. The protection and advancement of the common good in a context that recognises human rights. (163) 3rd

4. An evidence-based decision for the common good of society. (151) equal 4th

5. A decision-making process that is balanced and meets the needs of a majority of stakeholders. (151) equal 4th

6. The managed aggregation of interests depicted in the light of the need to reach consensus. (134) 5th

7. What matters to everyone in society in terms of their safety, welfare and wellbeing (at a given time). (125) 6th

8. Collective will expressed by law from an informed parliament. (124) 7th

9. A viewpoint that you reach at a point in time when you balance opposing evidence or viewpoints. (118) 8th

It is notable that the 'table technique' produced outcomes that were highly similar to the results of the NGT approach involving voting on the individual responses set out above. Using this data, the public interest could be defined in terms of *processes* and *goals*:

> *Processes*: The public interest contemplates evidence-based decisions for the common good of society and a decision-making process that is balanced and meets the needs of a majority of stakeholders. It involves the managed aggregation of interests depicted in the light of the need to reach consensus. It aims to achieve the collective will expressed through the laws passed by an informed parliament. It is a viewpoint that you reached at a point in time when opposing evidence or viewpoints are balanced.
>
> *Goals*: The public interest is characterised by decisions or actions for the common good of the relevant public, and a set of shared values that reasonably reflect those of the greater public, as reflected in the laws/rules of the group. The public interest is concerned with the protection and advancement of the common good in a context that recognises human rights, and what matters to everyone in society in terms of their safety, welfare and wellbeing (at a given time).

It is noteworthy that this distinction is the same one that Chris Wheeler describes in his analysis of the public interest.[24] Wheeler notes there are two main dimensions to the public interest: process/procedure; objectives/outcomes. We will return to this later in the paper. Another notable outcome from the table technique was that environmental concerns dropped out of the table discussions completely, although human rights emerged, and figured relatively prominently in the ultimate voting.

At the outset of the workshop we sought to respond to two research questions which, based on findings, we can now return to:

> **RQ1**. Can the public interest be defined in the abstract, that is, outside of specific decision-making contexts?

Based on the work of our group, we found that it is possible to develop a definition or series of definitions of the public interest. While many different *processes* were articulated by the group, it is possible to rank order those processes and develop typologies for decision-making based on them. Our second research question sought to dig deeper into the make-up, values and language proposed by our group:

> **RQ2**. Given the opportunity, will experts on the topic of the public interest define the concept by reference to a range of criteria and articulated values and, if so, what are they?

Based on the work of our group, we found that individuals and the table groups will define the public interest using a range of criteria and articulated values, set out in the findings above. This broadly affirms findings from the literature that, in the absence of an agreed definition, values that reflect social mores and concerns at the time will be used to describe and underpin how the concept of the public interest is understood.

Limitations

We noted earlier that our findings affirm Chris Wheeler's two broad dimensions of the public interest, that is: process/procedure and objective/outcomes. Wheeler notes that the objectives/outcomes dimension, which calls for 'identifying what is in the public interest in any given situation', is a primary obligation of public officials, involving an assessment of the relevant public, the relevant public interest issues, and the weighting of conflicts or competing interests.[25] What Wheeler's article clearly shows is that public interest definitions without these factors can simply provide guidelines which will ultimately call for further detail based on a 'publics-interests-conflicts' set of factors. In other words, while we have sought to ascertain a definition/s and values with no context, we acknowledge that in public use, the public interest will require these factors to be put into practice. We propose that the definitions and values developed here should be viewed as a theoretical framing of 'the public interest' that might then be used to assist in empirical or applied contexts.

Conclusions and further research

In this chapter, we have conducted a small experiment with a group of Australian experts with a strong interest in, and knowledge of, the concept of the public interest. Through our workshop, they were able to develop a series of theoretical definitions of the public interest, both individually and in larger groups. They were able to achieve consensus on processes and goals, and their relative importance, compared to each other. We do not propose generalising these definitions, as factors such as context, professional knowledge and issues of the day (both those covered at the symposium and those in the broader political, legal and social realms) would necessarily affect the data. What we have achieved, however, is a successful experiment interrogating the concept of the public interest within which informed and interested parties were able to reach consensus on priorities. This augurs well for the development of a possible future think tank on the topic, such as the one proposed by economist Ross Garnaut for the introduction of a 'Public Interest Council' to act as an independent, non-government body to coordinate debate on economic, social and political issues relating to the public interest.[26]

Finally, the value of NGT (and our modified version of it) is that the data produced for this chapter can be used to develop a survey instrument that will have content and construct validity. In our quest to develop qualitative data on this topic, that will be our next goal.

★ ★ ★ ★

Appendix

List of definitions provided by individuals and tables at the symposium

1. How and why we make decisions for a larger society – not necessarily at state or national level but the majority.
2. Acts or decisions that advance the public good, without unfairly prejudicing sectional or individual interests.
3. Transparent decisions based on policy to benefit most as opposed to the few.
4. Decisions or actions for the common good of the relevant public.
5. The shared/agreed set of beliefs/views/values that reasonably represent those of the 'public' group, often set out in the 'laws/rules' of that group.
6. An interest that accommodates the greatest good for the greatest number of people without breaching any law or humanitarian

obligation. OR an interest that accommodates public will without breaching any law or humanitarian obligation.

7. The right of the 'overall public' to be informed, to participate in (where feasible) to have transparent decision-making that is fair, equitable and accountable (my difficulty is defining 'public interest' as opposed to sectional interests. There can be diverse interests).

8. 'The public interest' takes us to the high ground of decision-making; due process, and the avoidance of conflicts. In respect of the outcomes we seek it must start with the majority view as expressed in an election. Also involved must be concern for the future (and the past/as well as the present, concerns for minorities as well as the majority and respect for social and environmental factors as well as economic if it is to be truly 'public', that is to say representative of all and not just some of us.

9. The aggregated shared aspirations and common ambitions of the undifferentiated population which are the focus and goal of public policy and procedure.

10. Ecologically sustainable development.

11. Collective benefit.

12. That which is of benefit to the population as a jurisdiction (it is distinct from the will of the people).

13. Acting in the interest of the many.

14. The process of engaging with affected and interested parties to determine an acceptable course of action to address an issue.

15. The pursuit of a common good through just means.

16. The common good/community interest – sustainable community interest.

17. The will of the community expressed by law, passed through a properly informed elected parliament, administered through a consultative public source using transparent guidelines.

18. An ideology reflecting benefit or positive outcomes, across domains, to the population/general public.

19. Any policy, process or program that positively impacts the safety and well-being of the collective/nations/citizens.

20. Public interest is a placemarker that prevents decisions from being made solely in the interests of the parties/decision-makers/stakeholders/those directly involved in the decision. It generalises decision-making beyond purely private interests.

21. The collective interests of a cohort of individuals which advance (or the fulfilment of which advances) the group or constituency's wellbeing.

22. The maintenance or advancement of a society's economic, social, cultural aspects in order to benefit the greatest number.

23. Something that may positively or negatively impact the public/society as a whole.

24. A conclusion/view reached in a disputed/contentious/unresolved issue of more than individual concern, after all relevant matters have been considered and balanced.

25. Rational decision-making processes and outcomes arrived at democratically by an informed electorate that serves the electorate.

26. Rational decision-making processes and outcomes arrived at democratically by an informed electorate.

27. That which is done that has potential to benefit or disadvantage the people as a whole – or a subset of the whole – in terms of their social, material or other relations.

28. Safety, wellbeing, welfare, national prosperity – not political expediency and slogans.

29. An interest that is neither personal or political, that affects someone or something related to Australian policy.

30. A decision made for the common good of society without inflicting/minimising harm to individuals or groups, made in support of shared values (such as the Universal Declaration of Human Rights).

31. A decision or action which is in the greater/common good, is lawful, procedurally fair and transparent.

32. For the good of the broader community as a whole – not just private interests.

33. The shared wants of citizens in a nation that warrant democratic politicians to advocate for such wants.

34. The public interest is that which is morally, ethically, and practically good and right for the majority of peoples.

35. For the benefit of the community/affecting everyone.

36. The public interest is a decision-making process for the benefit of the majority of a society.

37. Is policy or legislation for the common good of society/public.

Endnotes

1   F J Sorauf, 'The public interest reconsidered', *The Journal of Politics*, vol. 19, no. 4, 1957, p. 617.

2   Sorauf, 'The public interest reconsidered', p. 617.

3   P Herring, 'Public Interest', in David L Sills (ed.), *International Encyclopedia of the Social Sciences,* 1968, New York: Macmillan Co and Free Press, 1968, p. 170.

4   B Bozeman, *Public values and public interest: counterbalancing economic individualism,* Georgetown University Press, Washington DC, 2007 p. 84.

5   C Wheeler, 'The public interest revisited – We know it's important but do we know what it means?' *AIAL forum 48*, 2012, p. 12.

6   See, for example, FJ Sorauf 1957; JAW Gunn, 'Interests will not lie: a seventeenth century political maxim', *Journal of the History of Ideas*, vol. 29, no. 4, 1968, pp. 551–64; TM Benditt, 'The public interest', *Philosophy and Public Affairs*, vol. 2, no. 3, 1973, pp. 291–311; RE Flathman, *The Public Interest: An Essay Concerning the Normative Discourse of Politics,* John Wiley & Son, New York, 1966; A Downs, 'The public interest: its meaning in a democracy', *Social Research,* vol. 29, no. 1, 1962, pp. 1–36.

7   B Bozeman 2007; C Wheeler 2013; M Carter A Bouris, *Freedom of information: balancing the public interest,* 2nd edn, The Constitution Unit-University College, London, 2006; Tom Frame, *Who Defines the Public Interest?* Connor Press, Brisbane; J. Johnston, *Public Relations & the Public Interest,* Routledge, New York, 2016.

8   B Mitnick, 'The public interest', in RW Kolb (ed.), *Encyclopedia of Business Ethics and Society*, Los Angeles, Sage, 2008, p. 1735.

9   C Elliott, 'The readers' editor … how should we define the public interest', *The Guardian,* 21 May 2012, Retrieved from <https://www.theguardian.com/commentisfree/2012/may/20/open-door-definition-public-interest>; Lord Justice Leveson, *An inquiry into the culture, practice and ethics of the press*, 29 November, 2012, at <http://www.levesoninquiry.org.uk>.; Mitnick 2008.

10   Lord Justice Leveson, *An inquiry into the culture, practice and ethics of the press*, 29 November 2012, at <http://www.levesoninquiry.org.uk.>. p. 236.

11   Bozeman, *Public values and public interest*; Carter & Bouris, *Freedom of information*, 2006.

12   *D v National Society for the Prevention of Cruelty to Children*, [1978] AC 171, at 230.

13   Leveson, *An inquiry into the culture, practice and ethics of the press*, p. 1684.

14   Elliott 'The readers' editor'; Flathman, *The Public Interest*; Leveson, *An inquiry into the culture, practice and ethics of the press*; R Garnaut, *Dog Days: Australia After the Boom*, Redback, Melbourne, 2013.

15   Elliott, 'The readers' editor'; Johnston, *Public Relations & the Public Interest*.

16   AL Delbecq & AH VandeVen, 'A Group Process Model for Problem Identification and Program Planning', *Journal of Applied Behavioral Science*, 7, 1971, pp. 466–91.

17   JM Bartunek & JK Murnighan, 'The nominal group technique: Expanding the basic procedure and underlying assumptions', *Group and Organization Studies*, 9, 1984, pp. 417–32.

18   V Totikidis, 'Applying the Nominal Group Technique (NGT) in Community Based Action Research for Health Promotion and Disease Prevention', *The Australian Community Psychologist*, vol. 22 no. 1, 2010, pp. 18–29.

19   P Keyzer, J Johnston, M Pearson, S Rodrick, & A Wallace, 'The courts and social media; what do judges and court workers think?' *Judicial Officers' Bulletin*, vol. 25 no. 6, 2013, pp. 45–51.

20   Interaction Design Foundation, 'Learn how to use the best ideation methods: brainstorming, braindumping, brainwriting and brainwalking', <https://www.interaction-design. org/literature/.

21   This is the major benefit of the NGT technique, see Keyzer et al 2013.

22   Schram 2006; NK Denzin, *Interpretive interactionism (2nd ed.)*, Sage, Thousand Oaks, CA, 1989.

23   TH Schram, *Conceptualizing and proposing qualitative research*, (2nd ed.), Upper Saddle River, New Jersey: Pearson Education, 2006, p. 7.

24   Wheeler, 'The public interest revisited'.

25   Wheeler, 'The public interest revisited', p. 48.

26   Garnaut, *Dog Days: Australia After the Boom*.

CHAPTER 3

Civitas to pub test

Andrew Blyth

S cholarly attention focusing on the concept of the public interest has evolved steadily over the last four decades. Much of this work, produced by academics, policy researchers, political practitioners, bureaucrats, industry groups, and think tanks, demonstrates a rise in the use of the concept. Further interest has come from print media journalists, parliamentarians, radio personalities, cartoonists, Internet bloggers, subscription television broadcasters, comedians and satirists. Despite its ubiquity in these media, their practitioners have not used it with any greater precision. This chapter traces the evolution of the public interest – from its origins in Roman times to modern Australia – arguing that we are no closer to a definition and the concept is at risk of becoming little more than a cliché.

Civitas to common good

Civitas is an ancient Roman concept rich in history and influence. Grounded in the foundation of the Roman republican polity and social culture, the term signifies the rights and privileges of citizens. In areas of the empire that were newly under Roman rule, such a *civitas* encompassed a citizenry, council and magistrates, and a set of procedural rules adaptable to local custom. In many cases there was encouragement to form a city to provide a physical setting for the new institutions. The next step was sometimes for its officials to link with representatives of the Roman state, such as provincial governors.[1] A range of writers have commented favourably on ancient Greek and Roman experiences of political freedom and of citizens belonging to a political community (*polis*) within which they exercised the rights of citizenship (*civitas*).[2] Fully participating in the *polis* was thought to be the greater ideal and 'the crown of human activity'.[3]

The work of two scholars who have focused on the origins of civil society deserve close attention. The seminal publication, *The World of the Citizen in Republican Rome*, by the French historian, Claude Nicolet (1930–2010), offered readers a unique insight into the civic life of the Roman Republic.[4] Tracing the origins of *civitas* and drawing on both Greek and Latin interpretations, Nicolet discusses the rights, activities and obligations of the Roman citizen before introducing the notion of the 'integrated citizen'. Nicolet contends that the average Roman was not merely subject to professional politicians but was actively engaged in Rome's institutional structures and corporate life. Peter Hawkins, Professor in Religious Studies at Yale University, approached *civitas* through a religious lens. Writing of its extraordinarily rich meaning with roots deep into the common life of the people, Hawkins contends

> [f]or the Romans, to speak of *civitas* was to point to the communal reality that coheres within a city's walls and which unites its outlying territories by a common ethos of principle and association. What it represented, therefore, was a consensus more than a constitution: it offered the city a shared lexicon of words, gestures, images and dreams.[5]

Historical analyses of Rome's decline are well documented.[6] Despite Cicero's argument of decay and Augustine's thesis of a citizenry lacking virtue, the culture of antiquity and its resulting economic, legal, and administrative institutions laid a traversable path from the ancient to the medieval worlds. In the twilight of the *polis*, and the resulting collapse of *civitas Romana*, the concept of the 'common good' gained currency among philosophers and theologians.

During the 15th and 16th centuries, the common good was one of several important themes considered by theorists of political thought and practice. The notion gained momentum through the writings of Saint Thomas Aquinas' who located the common good in the centre of his interpretations of the state and its civil purposes. He contended that all members of the political society needed to work together to assure good is pursued and attained. As the theologian, Richard A Crofts, explains:

> [i]n ... the first book of *On Kingship*, Thomas discussed the centrality of the common good in understanding the purpose of the state. All members of the political society must work together to assure that this good is achieved. The state must always exist not for the good of any individual or group of its citizens but for the good of all. The common good 'is the natural foundation for the being and the action of the state and the test of the justice of the laws the state enacts in the pursuit of its end'.[7]

In theory at least, Aquinas' preferred form of government was monarchy, more specifically supporting a limited or constitutional monarchy combining elements of monarchy, aristocracy, and democracy:

Accordingly, the best form of government is in a state or kingdom, wherein one is given the power to preside over all; while under him are others having governing powers; and yet a government of this kind is shared by all, both because all are eligible to govern, and because the rulers are chosen by all. For this is the best form of policy, being partly kingdom, since there is one at the head of all; partly aristocracy, in so far as a number of persons are set in authority; partly democracy, i.e., government by the people, insofar as the rulers can be chosen from the people, and the people have the right to choose their rulers.[8]

Aquinas' theoretical approach to state power emphasised the priority of several objectives, such as promoting peace, order, prosperity, justice and community. His political theory foregrounds the concept of the common good which the state, as the principal authority responsible for temporal affairs, must pursue. The practical application of Aquinas' work is not, however, without its challenges.[9]

The English philosopher, Thomas Hobbes (1588–1679), is rightly considered among the founders of modern political philosophy. Against the backdrop of political, religious, military and economic upheaval, Hobbes laid the foundation for modern political liberalism and representative government. His seminal treatise on politics, *Leviathan*, published in 1651, mainly concerns the structure of society and legitimate government. Hobbes' work on statecraft argues for a social contract and rule by an absolute sovereign. To avoid 'the war of all against all' Hobbes reasons for the establishment of strong and undivided government guaranteeing civil peace and social unity. The judgment of the crown was considered to represent the greater good of the community. The common good was treated as a higher good than of the apsirations of the individual. But the crown was soon found to be deficient.

Medieval feudalism and the rise of the national monarchies left a society with too little direction. Its weakest members were at the mercy of the strong. The pervasive force of the crown was being challenged. Dissent was afoot. England stood divided. A new direction was sought. A shift in language and conceptual thinking was apparent. The paternalism involved in the common good tradition no longer sat well with rising liberal tendencies in early modern Europe. The common good arguments – increasingly associated with the self-regarding and often unjustified demands of monarchies – was facing a new dawn. The individual was increasingly a factor in calculations of the public interest. Hobbesian thought centred on the essentially selfish human with individual interests acquired greater legitimacy. Hobbes radically undercut the bases of the traditional common good doctrine. Individualistic concepts of self-realisation emerged out of the arbitrary power, both the political power of the monarchs and the economic power of the aristocracy. A shift from communitarian emphases to the rising tide of individualism was taking hold.

The rise of the public interest

A shift in language from the 'common good' to the 'public interest' appears to have occurred in the academic literature from the 1960s. In the American spring of 1965, a new quarterly public policy journal was published by sociologist Daniel Bell and journalist Irving Kristol. *The Public Interest* focused on political economy and culture without being too concerned about foreign policy or the national interest. Drawing on Walter Lippmann's 1922 account of public opinion, the founding editors were clear about their guiding principle:

> We feel that a democratic society, with its particular encouragement to individual ambition, private appetite, and personal concerns has a greater need than any other to keep the idea of the public interest before it. Democracy, after all, is government by public opinion.

A similar shift in Australian scholarly writing is discernable from the early 1970s. Two years after the election of the Whitlam Government, London-educated political scientist, Hugh V Emy published his seminal work, *The Politics of Australian Democracy*.[10] Emy uses the terms 'common good' and 'public interest' almost interchangeably. Published in 1974 and a year before the 'dismissal' of the Whitlam Government, Emy positions public interest as a common good concept associated with government attempts to 'fashion policies in the interests of all'. As Emy observes

> [t]he concept of a common good, or public interest, stands for something other than the proviso that policies must enjoy (virtually) unanimous support. That may or may not be the case. The concept is more important because it expresses a significant part of the meaning inherent in a civil (or democratic) society: that people do have a common interest in the whole of which they are part, and that this interest is usually greater than the varying aims and desires which each has in isolation from one another.

He went on:

> If we appeal to 'the public interest' we mean that the government should respect the nature of 'the community' and the particular rights which members of the community claim in common and should conduct itself accordingly.

Emy was not alone advocating greater attention to the public interest. Many of the works published by Peter Self, a distinguished English-born academic at the Australian National University, also advanced understanding of public interest and its appeal as an arbiter in public policy. In his 1962 book *The State and the Farmer*, Self and Herbert Storing examined the notion of the public interest in the context of an emerging agricultural policy in the United Kingdom. A decade later, Self's *Administrative Theories and Politics*, published in 1972, further opened the concept to critical appraisal as a tool for executive decision-making. His commitment to exploring public interest theories in national economic solvency and environmental protection spanned more than 20 years.[11]

It is not until the first decade of the twenty-first century, however, that contributors to scholarship on the public interest broadened to include politicians and administrators. David Kemp, an academic political scientist and Liberal Party official before his election to Federal Parliament, has written extensively on public leadership and the public interest. Addressing the perceived crisis of leadership in Australian politics, Kemp argues that perception is not the reality. The problem, he contends, is that politics being conducted in the policy domain are often portrayed as something contrary to the public interest, resulting in a declining political culture. He highlights the need for political leaders with deep philosophical foundations who can devise public interest policies that resonate with the electorate.[12]

Chris Wheeler, a former deputy state ombudsman, has focused on administrative oversight, whistleblower protection, and the public interest.[13] He is concerned about the consistent application of the public interest in a post-privatisation landscape. With the conduct of public affairs no longer the domain of public servants, employees of private companies awarded government contracts must also apply a public interest test to their conduct. These 'seismic changes', according to Wheeler, 'have not been accompanied by a sufficiently expansive conversation about their wider consequences in terms of the public interest'.[14]

Australia21, self-promoted as a think tank for the public good, asked a group of individuals with varying backgrounds to address the question of *who* speaks for and *protects* the public interest.[15] The responses were varied. Former chief executive of Qantas and secretary of the Department of the Prime Minister and Cabinet, John Menadue, argues the lobbying power of vested interests has distorted the operation of government. Former Federal Leader of the Liberal Party and one-time UNSW economics professor, Dr John Hewson, decries the lack of leadership in policy reform. Reverend Elenie Poulos of the Uniting Church lays the blame for society's inequality and indifference to the public interest squarely on neo-liberalism. Former Foxtel boss and creative arts advocate, Kim Williams, speaks of the 'infantilisation' of Australian cultural and science policy as being two things that work against the public interest. Former Liberal Senator Fred Chaney suggests the 'win at all costs' approach in politics is inconsistent with the public interest and argues for greater public community engagement in the political process.

Another contributor argues the case for a national public interest council; while another overlooked the concept of 'the public interest' completely in wanting to advance Indigenous well-being.

Former state premier and academic, Geoff Gallop, claimed enthusiasm for the theory and practice of the public interest is writ-large. Describing the concept as 'indispensable' in a destabilising world, Gallop illustrates the seriousness of the public interest to national life by listing a number of elements he considers may be helpful to public officials: engaging with people through more direct forms of democracy, incorporating checks and balances into law making and government, using research to inform decision-making, adopting strategic planning, incorporating the sustainability principle, and adopting a respectful regard for history. Gallop calls for elected and non-elected officials in government to think about means as well as ends, to broaden their understanding of which interests matter most, and the pursuit of good government as both a cause and an effect of the public interest. This body of work is developing alongside rising populism in Australia leading to the polarising of debate, political disconnection with public opinion, and continuing decline in the public's trust of vital state and social institutions.[16]

Lurching towards the 'pub test'

The 'public interest' is a fluid concept within Western parliamentary democracy, including Australia.[17] Sir William Lyne, the first Australian Minister for Home Affairs, spoke of the public interest during a debate in the House of Representatives in June 1901 in dealing with the national outlook; Winston Churchill invoked the public interest in his first speech as the British Prime Minister in the House of Commons in May 1940 when speaking of national objectives; and Malcolm Fraser in parliamentary Question Time asserted the public interest in defence of his government's policy in 1976 when addressing obstacles to fulfilling national destiny.[18] The meaning has clearly evolved over time as the public interest has been cited regularly as the basis for all kinds of government action. The circumstances have also expanded with governments of all political persuasions explaining their more unpopular decisions in terms of serving or protecting the public interest. The public interest is often used to imply neutrality and altruism.

The language of the public interest has also morphed into the less formal idiom of 'the pub test'. Taking the temperature of an issue and describing the collective opinion of ordinary Australians now dominates the modern political landscape. The colloquial 'pub test' has evolved over the last 20 years from the pages of print media and radio to digital television screens.[19] Along with the 'supermarket stroll' and 'talk-back tirade', the 'pub test' conjures up images of members of the public casting a suspicious eye over public policy with their considered judgments, if they deserve to be called that, likely to be revered. Not surprisingly, and quite appropriately, the 'pub test' has also been the subject of parody.

The long-running 'Clarke and Dawe' segment on ABC television hosted by the late John Clarke and Bryan Dawe has taken aim at the veracity of the pub test.[20] Its format is a mock studio-based interview conducted by the two hosts on a matter of public importance. In promoting the weekly sketch on its social media page, the ABC asks its audience to consider whether 'there couldn't be a fairer test' than asking someone about a policy in a pub – the social centre in the lives of many Australians. In the five-minute sketch, Clarke parodies then-Treasurer Scott Morrison discussing company tax cuts at a local pub with then-Prime Minister Malcolm Turnbull. The interviewer quickly deduces the pair had simply asked *each other* about the proposed tax cuts surrounded by people 'having a few (drinks)'. The then-Treasurer claims euphorically the company tax cuts have *indeed* passed the pub test.

In another parody, comedian Kitty Flanagan offers a questionnaire to patrons at a pub as part of ABC television's *The Weekly with Charlie Pickering*. Flanagan tries to persuade Pickering that her 'actual pub test' is a measure of what is acceptable to patrons; challenging whether politicians really enter a pub to ascertain the views of their constitutents or merely 'imagine' what the people who vote for them think. After canvassing popular opinion from the common 'drinking man (and woman)' on politicians' travel expenses, Flannagan summarises the 'results' of the test. She shows footage of some patrons (who are actors) stumbling as they hand back the completed questionnaire while others are sleeping at the bar and show no interest in any political issue. At the end of the segment, Flannagan triumphantly declares *her* 'pub test' is a 'good gauge of public opinion'. It is essentially uninformed or indifferent.

In contrast to the satire and comedy featured on the ABC, there is a serious attempt to critique policy via the 'pub test' on Foxtel's 'Paul Murray Live'. Hosted by former Sydney radio announcer, Paul Murray, a series of 'Pub Test' specials were aired during the 2019 Federal Election campaign. Political candidates were 'tested' on their party's policies by members of a live audience gathered in pubs and clubs throughout regional Australia. In promoting the uniqueness of the televised 'pub test', Paul Murray contends

> [t]his isn't the Paul Murray Show – it's *The Pub Test* [emphasis added].
> It's about the people asking the questions that matter to them. This is
> true live television, unpredictable and dangerous for MPs or aspiring
> MPs who think they can just float through with slogans.[21]

Confirming the standing of the 'pub test' as a means of gauging community sentiment and an indicator of the public interest, the program recorded its highest ratings with the pub test specials.[22]

Conclusion

The concept of the 'public interest' and the term the 'pub test' have an elevated role in political discussion in modern Australia. Policies determining Australia's trillion-dollar economy are no longer the sole domain of parliamentarians arguing for and against a policy in the Federal Parliament. Policies are now subjected to the opinions of pub patrons; a test disparaged by commentators and satirised by entertainers. Recent newspaper headlines suggesting that Scott Morrison's re-election strategy relied heavily on him and his policies passing the 'pub test' ought to be a cause for concern.[23] The need for the conduct of serving and former parliamentarians to pass a 'pub test' to determine whether they have been either truthful or honest is equally concerning.[24] The 'pub test' appears to be suffering from definitional 'bracket creep'. No longer is the test the weather vane for government policy. It seems to have been extended and applied to all political activity. The ignorant are often asked to stand in judgment of the informed.

While no-one could seriously suggest prohibiting use of the 'pub test' to gauge the public interest, its uncritical use has potentially cheapened the conduct of Australian politics. Depictions of the public interest are susceptible to manipulation if the 'pub test' is promoted as an egalitarian, anti-elitest strategy for determining what matters to the bulk of the population. Lumping policy and opinion together is mistaken. Very often people want things that are contrary to their interests; indeed, they may be harmful despite whatever appeal or allure they might have when viewed from a certain angle.

The quality of public debate is shaped by the language people use and the concepts used to evaluate rival claims and competing conclusions. While the founders of the journal, *The Public Interest*, asserted that democracy is ultimately government by public opinion, the pub test is no substitute for careful sifting of evidence and conscientious sorting of argument, activities that are intregral to any reasoned and responsible depiction of the public interest. Appealing as it is to populists, the pub test is not a reliable guide to good public policy or an indicator of what matters, and ought to matter, to a society determined to meet the needs of all its people. The satirists and comedians have exposed the flaws and fallacies of the latest attempt at mob rule.

Endnotes

1   See *Oxford Dictionary of the Classical World*, Oxford University Press, 2007: https://www.oxfordreference.com/view/10.1093/acref/9780192801463.001.0001/acref-9780192801463-e-479.
2   PGW Glare, *Oxford Latin Dictionary*, Clarendon Press, Oxford, 1968.
3   See Andreas Buss, 'The Evolution of Western Individualism', *Religion*, 2000, no. 30, pp. 1–25.
4   Claude Nicolet, *The World of the Citizen in Republican Rome* (translate by PS Falla), University of California Press, 1980, pp. 17–49.
5   See Peter Hawkins, *Civitas: Religious Ideas of the City*, Scholars Press, 1986, p. xii.
6   David Hollenbach, 'The Common Good Revisited', *Theological Studies*, 50, 1989, p. 80 cited. https://journals.sagepub.com/doi/pdf/10.1177/004056398905000104.
7   Gerald J Lynam in *The Good Political Ruler according to St. Thomas Aquinas*, Washington, 1953, p.3 cited in Richard A Crofts, 'The Common Good in the Political

Theory of Thomas Aquinas', *The Thomist: A Speculative Quarterly Review*, vol. 37, no. 1, January 1973, pp. 155–73.

8   Richard A Crofts, 'The Common Good in the Political Theory of Thomas Aquinas', p. 162.

9   Crofts, 1973, p. 172.

10   See Hugh V Emy, *The Politics of Australian Democracy: An Introduction to Political Science*, Macmillan, Melbourne, 1974.

11   See John Uhr, 'The Public Interest and Public Sector Priorities' paper presented at 'The Public Interest: Exploring Definitions and Assessing Difficulties' conference held by UNSW Canberra, 9–10 May 2018.

12   David Kemp, 'Crisis of leadership and philosophy' [online], *Meanjin*, vol. 74, no. 3, Spring 2015: 23–26. Availability:<https://search.informit.com.au/documentSumm ary;dn=620463440342533;res=IELLCC> ISSN: 0025–6293, cited 4 July 2019.

13   See https://www.ombo.nsw.gov.au/news-and-publications/publications/speeches/ speeches-by-the-deputy-ombudsman-chris-wheeler.

14   See Chris Wheeler's discussion paper in UNSW Canberra and NSW Ombudsman Public Interest Symposium booklet, 'The Public Interest: Exploring Definitions and Assessing Difficulties', 9–10 May 2018.

15   *Who speaks for and protects the public interest in Australia: Essays by notable Australians*, Australia21 Limited, 2015.

16   Speech by then Leader of the Opposition, John Howard, discussing decline in trust, *Headland Speech*, June 1995; and, Edelman Trust Barometer 2017 https://www. edelman.com/post/australia-trust-in-tumult, accessed 25 September 2018.

17   My thanks to Alan Wilson, former parliamentary librarian and volunteer at the Howard Library, for conducting a search of the National Library of Australia's online library database, *Trove*. This search revealed that the phrase 'common good' was used in Australia's first newspaper, the *Sydney Gazette and New South Wales Advertiser*, on 28 August 1803. The phrase, 'public interest', appeared in the 25 May 1806 issue of that newspaper.

18   Commonwealth of Australia, Parliamentary Debates, House of Representatives, 27 June 1901, https://parlinfo.aph.gov.au/parlInfo/search/display/display.w3p;adv=yes;or derBy=customrank;page=2;query=Dataset:hansardr,hansardr80%20Decade:1900s%20 Year:1901%20Content:%22public%20interest%22;rec=8;resCount=Default; Churchill speech in House of Commons, https://winstonchurchill.org/resources/speeches/1940- the-finest-hour/blood-toil-tears-and-sweat-2/; and Commonwealth of Australia, Parliamentary Debates, House of Representatives, 18 February 1976, https://parlinfo. aph.gov.au/parlInfo/search/display/display.w3p;adv=yes;orderBy=customrank;page= 0;query=Dataset:hansardr,hansardr80%20Day:18%20Decade:1970s%20Month:02%20 Year:1976%20Content:%22public%20interest%22;rec=0;resCount=Default.

19   A search of the terms by Alan Wilson, 'common good', 'public interest', 'pub test', 'social capital', 'man in the street', and 'the average person' is revealing. Over the last two decades, the use of these terms by journalists, media commentators and par- liamentarians has rapidly increased. In the year 2000, the media's use of the 'public

interest' occurred on 998 occasions. By 2018, this figure rose to 2050. Over the same period, the use of the 'pub test' had risen 430 per cent. See Table 1.

20   Clarke and Dawe: 'Company tax cuts have passed the pub test', aired 6 April 2017, accessed at https://www.theguardian.com/media/2017/apr/10/john-clarke-10-best-clips-career-satire on 3 April 2019; https://www.facebook.com/abcnews.au/videos/clarke-and-dawe-scott-morrison-federal-treasurer/10156475108379988/; See Kitty Flannagan's 'Pub Test' spoof at: https://www.youtube.com/watch?v=aibcE2s51ro.

21   https://www.news.com.au/video/id-5348771529001−6025344192001/Warringah-candidates-face-the--pub-test--on-Paul-Murray-LIVE-.

22   https://www.smh.com.au/entertainment/tv-and-radio/sky-s-jump-to-the-right-has-boosted-ratings-but-at-what-cost-20190527-p51rlx.html; http://www.mcn.com.au/news/sky-news-delivers-record-q1-primetime-ratings.

23   'Scott Morrison, 'Board shorts and passing the pub test', and 'Scott Morrison's re-election strategy relies on him passing the 'pub test', are two recent examples: https://www.themonthly.com.au/today/paddy-manning/2018/21/2018/1545367209/pub-test-2018; https://www.smh.com.au/national/scott-morrison-board-shorts-and-passing-the-pub-test-20190114-p50ra2.html.

24   https://www.smh.com.au/politics/federal/doesn-t-pass-the-pub-test-wong-attacks-bishop-over-palladium-20190702-p523cw.html and https://indaily.com.au/news/2019/07/04/pm-seeks-advice-on-pyne-and-bishops-post-politics-jobs/.

Table 1
Results of Parl Info database search

phrase	common good				public interest				pub test				social capital				man in the street				the average person			
source	HR	Senate	Media	Australian	HR	Senate	Media	Australian	HR	Senate	Media	Australian	HR	Senate	Media	Australian	HR	Senate	Media	Australian	HR	Senate	Media	Australian
2000	5	6	81	16	131	156	998	196	1		1	2	16		145	16	1	1	17	12	11	3	78	29
2001	5	7	89	19	77	155	1182	214	1	1	6		5		115	19	3	2	23	9	11	3	77	26
2002	14	9	83	22	124	193	1166	225			3	1	12	8	96	22			20	7	13	1	73	22
2003	10	7	71	20	142	170	1105	211			1		25	10	187	20			16	5	11	7	81	23
2004	8	1	104	17	102	170	1291	190		2	5		12	3	164	17			13	10	5	4	77	21
2005	14	12	91	24	116	128	1468	245	2		11		7	9	132	24			36	5	12	7	147	28
2006	10	6	123	27	181	188	1540	303			3		7	4	117	27	2		38	8	7	4	148	26
2007	7	5	108	28	79	149	1318	309	2	1	10		2	4	79	28			36	11	3	2	183	32
2008	7	8	113	34	51	93	1277	368			33	4	6	6	90	34	1		36	18	10		178	19
2009	10	4	119	35	97	123	1261	345		1	1		21	6	93	35		1	24	9	11	5	155	28
2010	12	6	107	25	79	132	1487	424	2		3		6	2	61	25		1	30	5	8	3	164	18
2011	8	9	128	35	82	109	1737	436	2		4	1	8	3	124	35		1	44	18	15	1	147	38
2012	18	4	139	27	112	142	1966	485	4		11	3	10	6	125	27			29	9	9	4	180	23
2013	6	2	98	22	122	158	1913	440	1		49		10	1	84	22		1	35	6	8	3	201	23
2014	7	12	73	14	98	210	1220	289	1	1	52	12	7	2	74	14			10	3	10	3	97	21
2015	14	3	122	39	98	224	1267	386	3	10	199	32	6	3	87	39	2	1	18	3	4	3	165	22
2016	7	3	173	49	85	127	1413	389	2	6	141	28	2		84	49	1		29	6	6	5	161	20
2017	71	11	127	44	122	207	1634	665	15	19	401	93	12	1	86	44	1	1	18	3	3	9	247	24
2018	12	7	141	60	91	252	2050	705	5	6	430	74	8	3	104	60			22	6	7	4	213	25

63

CHAPTER 4

Public interest and competing interests

Chris Wheeler

A focus for the Ombudsman's office is decision-making in relation to complaints. This includes complaints made to that office about the actions of public authorities as well as complaints about its own performance. One of the key challenges is determining where to allocate resources. Which matters should be investigated? When should a complaint be referred back to an agency? How much time should be given to a particular issue? These questions become even more challenging when you are working with finite, and ever reducing, resources to respond to an increasing number of complaints. I have seen substantial changes to the complaint handling processes throughout the public sector over many years. Many of these have been very positive, with agencies dealing with more straightforward com-plaints effectively themselves without people needing to come to the New South Wales Ombudsman's office. This means that the office is seeing and becoming involved in the more complex matters and dealing with people who may present with more challenging behaviours and approaches.

One of the options that has been considered for ensuring continuing com-mitment to complaint handling and better service delivery is the creation of a legislative foundation for good customer service. A customer-service type act would require the government of the day to set a series of priorities for service provision. We see this including, among other things, a commitment to respond appropriately to all complaints. This sounds like a fairly simple concept, but it is not as easy as it seems. There are a very small number of people who, through their contact with and complaints to agencies, manage to consume an inordinate amount of service delivery and complaint handling resources. In some of these cases it is not an equitable or fair use, and other complainants may miss out because a louder, more demanding and more challenging voice has taken over. Here is a hypothetical example that is not an exaggeration:

> An individual makes a complaint to the health department about the way he/she is treated by a hospital. The person then raises his/her concerns with the relevant oversight body, and is not satisfied with the response. The person continues to contact that body repeatedly raising the same concerns. The person also continues to have contact with a wide range of health and emergency services. Each time one of these agencies comes into contact with the person, he/she makes a complaint or multiple complaints, and then escalate each complaint to the relevant oversight body. The person also emails each complaint to a wide range of government Ministers, both State and Federal, as well as members of Parliament and other State and Federal oversight bodies. The person does not accept the outcome of any of his/her complaints, and complains about the case officer who deals with each of their complaints as well as demanding a review of each matter. The person does not show any sign of slowing or changing behaviour, despite the efforts of the various frontline agencies and oversight and integrity agencies with which the person has had dealings.

While the ombudsman has guidance for agencies about how they can respond to what the office has termed unreasonable conduct by a complainant, in some cases people simply ignore these controls and continue to make contact and complain. Alternatively, the person may complain of discrimination and also start to make an 'access to information' application under the relevant legislative scheme. This is then followed by appeals to a tribunal about any refusal to provide access.

I was considering different ways to respond to such situations including a provision within a customer-service type Act to allow certain steps to be taken to manage a person's access to complaint handling services. This would be an approach where the consideration of the public interest would be essential. Where should limited resources be applied? How should a decision around a complaint management type order be made? Who should make that decision? How long should a restriction apply? These are all important questions and I am not suggesting we yet have the answers.

There are some equivalent provisions that may provide a useful starting point. In New South Wales, section 110 of the Government Information (Public Access) Act 2009 (Orders to restrain making of unmeritorious access applications) and the Vexatious Proceedings Act 2008 both provide for restrictions to control the making of information access applications and the ability to bring an action in court respectively. It is important to note that the Vexatious Proceedings Act was amended in recent years to allow for consideration of the conduct of individuals alone. This goes away from looking to the individual's intention and focusses on the resourcing impost of repeated proceedings. While the Act still has 'vexatious' in the title, motive is no longer the sole determining factor. These orders are placing restrictions on important rights in our society. Being able to make information access applications allows us to look behind government decision making and hold decision makers to account. Being able to access justice through the Court system is one of the central elements of our democracy, and restricting that access involves a substantial public interest balancing act.

These legislative provisions are aimed at ensuring a small percentage of people do not misuse two important accountability mechanisms. These provisions are not used lightly. From the cases we have encountered, they are only used in the most serious of cases. More thought is required as to how such a provision would operate in relation to complaints and people who make them. One possible approach would be to allow for a Tribunal (such as the New South Wales Civil and Administrative Tribunal) to make an order that allows an agency to apply a number of management strategies to respond to different types and seriousness of problems. These would be similar to the 'Civil Restraint Orders' made under the Civil Procedure Rules (UK). If this model were adopted, the next important public interest question is what kind of content, conduct, resourcing impacts and motive would trigger the use of such a restriction.

Some possible content considerations would be where complaints are submitted to an agency that:

- are repetitious in relation to their subject matter and the person or body the subject of complaint;
- contain clearly false or intentionally misleading statements of a significant nature relating to matters in contention;
- are made without reasonable grounds or are lacking in any substance;
- are so obviously untenable or manifestly groundless as to be utterly hopeless, misguided or misconceived; and/or
- are clearly delusional, imaginary, irrational, absurd or an exercise in futility (based on a 'reasonable person' type test).

In relation to conduct issues, criteria might include:

- the conduct of the complainant has raised significant work health and safety issues for the staff of an organisation;
- the number of complaints that have been made can reasonably be characterised as habitual, persistent or manifestly unreasonable in the circumstances;
- an unreasonable number of complaints have been made to the same person or organisation within a specific period;
- a number of complaints making allegations about the conduct or decisions of the same or related people or organisations raising substantially the same issues as in the previous complaints that were unsubstantiated (particularly if there has not been a significant interval in the time between them or significant changes in relevant circumstances).

In relation to resourcing issues, criteria might include that the number of previous or concurrent complaints made by the same complainant have substantially and unreasonably diverted the organisation's resources away from their use by the organisation in the exercise of its functions (similar to a ground in most access to information legislation for refusing to deal with a FOI/GIPA application).

In relation to motive issues, the criteria could be that the Tribunal was of the view, on reasonable grounds, that a complainant has frequently or persistently made complaints that appear to be made:

- to harass or annoy;
- to cause delay or detriment; and/or
- to achieve another wrongful purpose.

There are examples of restraint provisions beyond New South Wales. Under the Civil Procedures Rules (UK), a practice direction can be made which, among other things, sets out the circumstances where a court can make a civil restraint order against a party to the proceedings, and the consequences of such an order[1]. A supplementary practice direction on the making of the civil restraint orders contains provisions about the making of:

- *limited civil restraint orders* – 'where a party has made two or more applications which are totally without merit', preventing the party from 'making any further applications in proceedings in which the order is made without first obtaining the permission of the judge';
- *extended civil restraint orders* – 'where a party has persistently made claims or made applications which are totally without merit', preventing the party from 'issuing claims or making applications';
- *general civil restraint orders* – 'where a party against whom the order is made persists in issuing claims or making applications which are totally without merit', preventing the party from 'issuing any claim or making any application without the permission of the judge identified in the order'.

Once a decision has been made as to whether this is an appropriate approach to take, consideration will then be given to what such orders would look like. For example, the Tribunal making a decision might be authorised to:

- limit communications by a person by specifying:
  » the particular modes of communication the person can use to communicate with a named agency and its staff or a named official (for example letters delivered by Australia Post, emails, telephone or face to face interview);
  » the number of letters/emails/text messages the person can send to a named agency or official, telephone calls to any member of staff of a named agency or public official, or attendances at the premises of a named agency or official, in a specified time period;

> » the length of each allowable letter/email/text message (based on word count or pages), or length of each allowable telephone conversation or attendance at premises; and/or
> » the number of issues/allegations referred to in each such letter/email/text message, telephone conversation or interview.

· impose restrictions on access to the premises occupied by, and interactions with the staff of, a named agency or a named official.

· restrict disclosures/publication of certain information where the content of information previously published by the person on websites, blogs or other public social networking forums has been clearly misleading, defamatory, threatening, or the like, to the extent that it is reasonable to protect the health and/or safety of agency staff or other officials (similar to s.64 of the Civil and Administrative Tribunal Act 2013 (NSW)).

This is a particularly difficult area of public administration. On the one hand, we do not want to stop people from being able to come forward and raise their concerns about government actions and decision-making. This is an essential element of our system. On the other, a very small number of people should not be able to use and abuse the complaint handling process, using finite agency resources, placing undue strain on staff and preventing other people from having their concerns addressed. As one member of Parliament observed when the Vexatious Proceedings Bill was being introduced, the aim was to 'protect the fundamental right of citizens to approach the courts to seek justice in accordance with the law while preserving the efficiency of the justice system and shielding other participants in the justice systems from unmeritorious actions'. We are confronted here with a delicate balancing act, and it is a perfect example of the pivotal role the public interest serves in reaching a just, fair and reasonable outcome.

Endnotes

1   3.11 Power of the court to make a civil restraint order.
     A practice direction may set out –
       a. the circumstances in which the court has the power to make civil restraint order against a party to proceedings:
       b. the procedures where a party applies for a civil restraint order against another party; and
       c. the consequences of a court making a civil restraint order.

CHAPTER 5

Trust, politics and the public interest

Geoff Gallop

Trust is a most important word in our political vocabulary. It is used by political scientists to describe the state of relationships within government and between government and people and by political philosophers seeking values with which to anchor the ship of state in an ethical universe. I commence this chapter with a brief account of trust in Australian politcs today, noting that there are public policy initiatives such as deliberative democracy which are available to build better and more productive relationships in the system. I will then examine trust as a value, one of the two principles that underpin our system, the other being democracy. What trust requires of our politicians, particularly when they are privileged to be in government, will be put in the context of the political flexibility and strength needed to be effective in the pressured and contested world of personal ambitions, interests and ideologies.

Trust and relationships

The existence or otherwise of trust in the many relationships that form in and around government tells us a great deal about the state of governance in any jurisdiction. Efficiency and effectiveness in government depends on it. In this context, it is an analytical concept that can assist us in our empirical inquiries as political scientists. To illustrate this point, let me refer to four questions we might ask about government in general and about particular governments. First, do the people trust the government? Second, does the government trust the people? Third, does the government trust the public service? Fourth, do public servants trust the government? Studying and then commenting on politics and government with these questions in mind will tell us a good deal. If a well-researched answer to the questions is a resounding 'no', we can say with confidence that government will not be travelling well and, most importantly, will not be in a strong position to tackle the 'big issues' that necessarily provoke vested interests and substantial conflict. Indeed, distrust itself breeds conflict which can be debilitating and destructive.

Resting underneath this conclusion is a recognition of the importance of 'teams' and 'partnerships' in our public policy endeavours. Personal as well as political skills and capacities are crucial to good government. Not surprisingly, then, good schools of government ensure that issues like listening, negotiating and alliance-building are included, alongside conventional studies of structure and organisation.[1]

Also involved are important public policy questions relating to institutions that can build rather than undermine trust. For example, the current trust deficit often spoken about could be addressed not just by laws and regulations that seek a level playing field when it comes to issues like political donations and lobbying but also by more meaningful forms of public engagement, most notably the wider use of properly facilitated and randomly selected 'mini-publics' to recommend on policy. It might be a local issue requiring the equivalent of a jury or a much larger and complex question requiring an assembly and a lengthier time-line. Such techniques are being increasingly used by both the executive and legislative arms of government to assist in policy-making, not just because the decision-making involved has been found to be constructive and public interest oriented, but also because it helps re-build trust between people and government.[2]

Trust as principle

Add to these empirical concerns the place given to trust as one of the two foundation principles of government. In the *Second Report of the WA Inc. Royal Commission* (1992) the commissioners put it this way:

> Two complementary principles express the values underlying our constitutional arrangements. The first, the democratic principle, is

that: *It is for the people of the State to determine by whom they are to be represented and governed.*

This principle carries with it certain consequences. The first institution of representative government, the Parliament, must be constituted in a way which fairly represents the interests and aspirations of the community itself. The electoral processes must be fair. Public participation in, and support for, candidates, parties and programmes is to be encouraged. However, electoral laws should aim to prevent sectional interests from purchasing political favour, and to prevent those seeking election from attracting support by improper means.

The second, the trust principle, expresses the condition upon which power is given to the institutions of government and to officials, elected and appointed alike. It is that: *The institutions of government and the officials and agencies of government exist for the public, to serve the interests of the public.*

This principle in turn carries its consequences. It provides the 'architectural principle' of our institutions and a measure of judgment of their practices and procedures. It informs the standards of conduct to be expected of our public officials. And because it represents an ideal which fallible people will not, and perhaps cannot, fully meet, it justifies the imposition of safeguards against the misuse and abuse of official power and position.

Both principles, and the commitment which they assume to the rule of law and to respect for the rights and freedoms of individuals, need to be translated into practical goals if they are to provide the basis for government in this State.[3]

Talking about trust in this context takes us to the public interest and all of the institutions created to protect and promote it. It seeks of us reasonable behaviour, the rule of law, procedural fairness, being open to scrutiny, the avoidance of conflicts of interest and inappropriate discrimination, personal and institutional resistance to corruption, value for money and proper accountability arrangements overall.[4] It is one thing to have 'the numbers' and the power and authority it creates but all too often they are not used in the best interests of the people. So it is that, in our system, governments are 'subjected to accountability that is both imposed upon it from outside by the citizens, and accountability that is imposed upon itself through political institutions empowered to restrain the political executive.'[5]

In other words, we seek vertical accountability via free and fair elections and horizontal accountability by way of independent agencies like ombudsmen, auditors-general, administrative tribunals, human rights commissions and corruption commissions. They investigate, educate and deliberate on the basis of frameworks and definitions given to them by the legislature. Put simply, they bring principle to the exercise of power just as independent electoral commissions bring the principle of free and fair elections to the supervisory work they do. All of this has become part of the architecture of modern government, respected by most but questioned by others, most notably the 'whatever it takes' school of political practice.

Politics and principle

This leads me to ask whether or not there is an inherent conflict between politics and the principles defining the public interest. In order to examine this properly our starting-point ought to be a recognition that politics is, in and of itself, a good thing, the 'master science' as Bernard Crick called it in his 1962 classic, *In Defence of Politics.*

Politics is all about power and influence, making things happen in a real world of interests, ideologies and ambitions. These are the things that lead to pressure and perhaps deep and difficult discussions that sometimes cannot avert pure conflict. To make things happen the political skills associated with both 'soft' and 'hard' power are required. Judgment is required about when governments should shift gears from the former (soft) to the latter (hard). Indeed, judgment is required in dealing with all areas of government in a free society with its attendant pressures and conflicts. Negotiation and compromise are often the key factors for success (and for the maintenance of security and stability) in the real as opposed to an imagined world, assuming rationality can lead to faulty decisions. This is why Crick was opposed to all forms of fundamentalism, be they ideologically or technocratically inspired. Of Crick's approach, Andrew Gamble observed the following:

> Crick's point is that it is impossible to determine what the public
> interest is without trying to find out what it is that people want, and

how the different things they want can be reconciled. Only politics can do this. This means that democratic politics will often be scorned by many on left, right and centre because it is so messy, unprincipled, approximate and because politicians so often appear devious, evasive and untrustworthy.[6]

The conclusion I reach from all of this is that a good society needs an energetic and vibrant polity as well as skilled politicians – *and it is in the public interest* – that it be so. How, then, does this conclusion fit alongside the two principles of democracy and trust? Certainly, democracy needs politicians rather than ideologues or technocrats to make it work. But what of trust? Does it mean the standards it seeks set too high a bar if goals are to be achieved? This takes us to the age-old question – do the ends being sought justify the means chosen to achieve them?

Ends and means

There are two types of answer a skilled politician and political leader may give to this question. First, they will point to the real need for alliance-building, deal-making and compromise if things are to be done. Political leaders may claim a mandate but not have the numbers in the legislature. In this situation 'give and take' soon becomes the order of the day. They may find themselves up against powerful individuals or groups threatening campaigns if their interests are not met. Deeply-held and party-specific policies may have to be compromised and even worse, the government's very hold on power may be at stake. Favours are requested and often given. Time-line pressures may be at play, unhelpfully affecting proper process. In some circumstances, confidentiality (or at least evasiveness) may be required in the early days of negotiation. Mark Philp put it this way: 'Politicians often need room in which outcomes, probabilities, and policy can be explored and compromises hammered out without immediate exposure to the public gaze. Finding an agreement that will stick and that people can commit to often requires that the precise character of the bargaining is shielded from wider scrutiny or publicity.[7] Quite often, too, values themselves are in conflict, such as happens when local or national security needs come up against a belief in civil liberties.

Does all of that imply a dereliction of duty or is it 'the way of the political world'? Can we really expect of our politicians that they do not in any way think and act politically? It is the case, as Philp observes, that 'elements that are integral to winning, keeping, and exercising office sit together in an unstable and potentially conflicting mix with positional obligations, strategic political action and prudential behaviour.'[8]

> 'What we ignore at our peril', asserts the experienced politician, 'is the need
> for practicality and flexibility and their twins, adaptability and agility.'

Second, there are situations where stalemates exist, crisis looms large and decisions are needed, but nothing is happening. Here we see the deal-making and negotiation associated with politics incapable of delivering results for the community. This takes us to executive power and the judgment required to ensure it is used to good effect as is required in our tripartite system involving legislature, executive and judiciary. Leaders often find themselves driven to act 'for reasons of state' and in ways that lead to questioning from others as to whether or not the power is being used legitimately and the requirements of due process are being respected as we would normally expect.

> 'What we ignore at our peril', asserts the experienced leader, 'is the need
> for strength in the face of systemic failure or crisis.'

I was in such a situation when faced with evidence of sexual abuse of children in an Aboriginal community led by a leading activist for Indigenous causes, Robert Bropho. The evidence had surfaced in the Coronial Inquest into the suicide of a 15-year-old at the camp and by way of an *Inquiry into Responses by Government Agencies of Complaints of Family and Child Abuse in Aboriginal Communities* established by my Government and chaired by a magistrate, Sue Gordon.

It was clear that the normal methods of ensuring accountability were not working and that anything less than legislation and the complete closure of the camp would be inadequate. This raised challenging issues related to rights, but also a moral imperative to act decisively in order to free women and children who were, in effect, trapped by the power structures and fences that existed. Legislation to close the camp was enacted and, as Premier, I put into place an administrator. My actions were criticised as being racist. I never believed these criticisms were either accurate or fair. It was a personal relief when my actions, which were assessed by the Federal Court, were deemed reasonable and justified.[9] A majority view of a Legislative Council Select Committee was nonetheless critical, complaining that I had by-passed 'normal processes' to achieve the result.[10] Robert Bropho was eventually brought to justice in 2005 and again in 2008. He was found guilty of the abuse of children under care dating from the 1990s, the youngest being an 11-year-old. The Judge described his crimes as 'the lowest form of abuse imaginable'.[11]

What this reference to 'flexibility' and 'strength' tells us is that real-world tensions exist between politics and the public interest. It is not that there is inevitable conflict between the two. Politics is not corrupt. At the most fundamental level, it is simply the contest of ideas. But politics can be corrupting when governments push the boundaries in the interests of outcomes they see as necessary.[12] Governments will seek to do all they can, and sometimes more, to secure not only their power and their policies but also peace and security for the community they represent. It is complicated, too, by the logic of democracy and the requirement we place on governments to keep their promises. The question becomes: 'when is this behaviour consistent with the public interest and when is not it?'

> 'Surely,' pleads the Prime Minister, Premier or Chief Minister, 'we have a mandate to govern because of the victory we achieved at an election. Indeed, don't we have a right to govern? Don't we have an obligation to do whatever it takes to deliver on our commitments?'

We are left with the question as to whether these political and practical considerations undermine what we believe to be the public interest as outlined by bodies like the WA Inc. Royal Commission. The reality is that what is and is not acceptable behaviour has an element of judgment attached to it. Note, too, that there is also disagreement over the very standards we incorporate into legislation and over the powers we give to the various agencies of accountability. Just as politicians may push themselves beyond the boundaries of acceptability in order to get things done, so may they, when acting as legislators, limit those boundaries in ways that thwart and undermine the open-ended practice of politics. This is not an uncomplicated good versus bad scenario.

Nor can we say that what we might regard as unacceptable behaviour by an individual in their daily lives would be seen as such in the real world of politics. Circumstances can change quickly. Those who were once friends may fall out and even become enemies. True believers may be left stranded and disillusioned as their party drops long-held commitments for short-term political gains. Elections in particular can bring out the worst in people as they manoeuvre for support and engage in high level spin to exaggerate their strengths and the other side's weaknesses. It is important, then, that we do not allow such concerns about personal morality to take over our definition of what it is to act consistently with the public interest. It would set the bar in ways impossible to achieve. Politics is not free of ethical considerations but they slot in differently to other areas of human endeavour. Political life is not an uncomplicated saint versus sinner scenario.[13]

The public service and ministerial offices

It is unrealistic to examine these matters without reference to two other institutions that come into play in the daily lives of an elected government – the public service and the ministerial office. Indeed, it is often argued that the rise in prominence of the latter, both absolutely and relatively, poses a threat to the public interest, particularly when coupled with an increasingly politicised public service. It has been labelled as the 'New Public Governance' that involves 'the integration of executive governance and the continuous campaign, partisan political staff as a third force in governance and public administration, a personal politicisation of appointments to the senior public service, and an assumption that public service loyalty to, and support for, the government means being promiscuously partisan for the government of the day'.[14] If it is all politics, so the argument goes, who is going to speak truth to power when it is needed? If it is all politics, who is going to speak for evidence?

It all goes back to United States' President Woodrow Wilson's insight that the public service cannot be a 'mere instrument' of the elected government, its responsibilities are broader than that and what is required as a result is a sound knowledge of what the law allows and does not allow and what administrative realities tell us about what can and what cannot be achieved with the resources available. It is central to their role, Wilson wrote, to 'seek to straighten the paths of government, to make its business less unbusiness-like, to strengthen and purify its organisation, and to crown its duties with dutifulness.[15] It is not just that they have this role but that they are also well-placed to undertake it. Public servants work at the pointy end of government. While it is to be expected that political advisers in the minister's office should know about law, evidence and practicality, it is unlikely that they will have the background, knowledge and experience of the well-credentialled public servant.

The province of the staffer lies in ensuring that political considerations are brought to the table of decision when considering public policy. It is often observed there are three questions we may ask of all policy. First, is there evidence it can work to achieve the objectives? Second, are the resources, including public service capacity, available to make it happen? Third, does it have community acceptance?[16] The last question is not just an optional extra but goes to the heart of whether change can be achieved – and sustained into the future. That takes us to all sorts of political considerations. Are the numbers in the parliament? will there be community backlash and orchestrated campaigns opposed to proposed changes? Is the extra-parliamentary party on side? How is the government going to communicate its message? Good governments will take these questions seriously and it is the function of a ministerial office to see to it that this is the case, along with managing the minister's work more generally.

Political reality is such that the temptations are many for ministers and their staff to cross the line between what is and is not acceptable in the way they relate to the public service. There is relevant distinction to be made here between politics and administration. It is not clear cut and never easy to apply but it is there nevertheless. In our public service legislation, we require of heads of department that they manage equitably and with consistency. When it comes to appointments that means merit and when it comes to the administration of policy that means no special favours. For these things they are held accountable and it follows that the political and legal capacity to speak truth to power is required when the blurring of responsibilities raises public interest considerations.[17]

So much goes on behind-the-scenes in the minister's world, and within his or her office and the across public service. Ministers may be under pressure from marginal seat holders or cross-bench parliamentarians, they need supporters and resources for their re-election campaigns, and lobbyists of all sorts will come knocking on their door. The pure politics in all of this may swamp them such that power and its exercise in the interests of the minister and/or his or her political party becomes an end-in-itself and it is why, in New South Wales, a part of a definition of corruption in section 8 (1) (a) the *Independent Commission Against Corruption (ICAC) Act* includes conduct that 'could adversely affect, either directly or indirectly, the honest or impartial exercise of official functions by any public official or any public authority'. Ministers or their staffers may seek personal information about opponents, they may seek 'jobs for the boys', and they may seek favours when it comes to the allocation of resources. They may get into the habit of going around the departmental head and forging partnerships with public servants seen as supportive of their party and its agenda.

This reminds us that otherwise cogent and convincing arguments about the need for executive power, confidentiality and narrowly political considerations for our system to work may become effectively little more than an excuse to cover up bad practices, impropriety and even corruption. Yes, ministerial staffers are 'political' in their purposes; they seek to support their boss in his or her role but like the minister and the public service it is now understood that they are not free of obligations to the public interest. To this end it is important that they be provided with a legislative framework that outlines roles and responsibilities and is backed up with agreed protocols for working with the public service and an appropriate code of conduct around which professional development programs can be developed.[18]

Stronger standards/ more accountability

I have stressed that there is no easy answer to the dilemmas associated with ends and means but we do have the standards the community sets for itself and incorporates into relevant legislation. Such standards inform us where and when alarm bells should ring and where further, more intensive inquiries to be conducted by, for example, a corruption commission, may be needed. What contemporary politicians need to understand is that the standard of impropriety or even corruption may not be limited to criminal behaviour brought to account in a courtroom, but will be broader in aspiration and definition, including items like 'partiality' and 'breach of trust'.

What is different about the accountability climate today, however, is not just a wider definition of what is expected, but also more powerful machinery to uncover 'the truth of the matter'. In this context, two institutions come to mind – human rights commissions that can indicate whether or not laws, regulations, policies and actions violate our human rights and corruption commissions which report to parliament on whether or not corruption has occurred and whether a referral to the Director of Public Prosecutions (DPP) is merited.

In other words, rather than just rely on the parliament, occasional commissions of inquiry and the media, we have added new agencies of accountability to the picture. Their role is to inquire and report, thus adding to what we understand to be 'the facts' of the matter. Where there are charters of rights in Victoria, the Australian Capital Territory and Queensland, they can indicate breaches, but do not have the power to overturn laws as is the case with a formal Bill of Rights. Where there are corruption commissions their role is also to inquire and report to parliament, the role of the DPP being to determine whether or not prosecution should follow. I make this point conscious that such bodies have a wider educative and preventive role as well.[19]

Back, then, to the requirements seen as essential by our experienced politician and leader – practicality, flexibility and strength. They remain intact as elements needed for democracy to work but when expressed in ways that raise ethical questions, more serious regimes of accountability are in place to examine and report. It remains the case that individual parliamentarians, party leaders, parliament and, ultimately, the people themselves, are left to judge whether or not political follow-up is required following a report from an agency empowered to investigate. On the one hand, individuals and even chief ministers and their governments may resign and non-elected officials may resign or be demoted. On the other hand, they may seek to tough it out, even when the findings are clear-cut or the upper houses of parliament are not on side. What is important is that in such circumstances all of the relevant facts are on the table and that the agencies created to find them are themselves professional and accountable. They, too, are expected to act in the public interest.

Indeed, it is the creation of these new and powerful fact-gathering agencies that is the contemporary solution to the tension between real world politics and the public interest. Politicians, their staffers and public servants may regret this extra intrusion into their decisions and decision-making but they ignore it at their own peril. What they do and why they do it will, more likely than not, be fully exposed. It is part of our system today, but not the only part, and they need to be reminded that there are still many ways in which power can be won and influence exercised without permanent harm to the trust required for our system to work effectively.

Endnotes

1   Geoff Gallop, 'Leadership - It's all about you', in Philip Crisp (ed.), *So You Want to be a Leader*, Hybrid Publishers, Melbourne, 2015, pp. 23–31.

2   Geoff Gallop, 'Helping our Democracy Work Better', *Meanjin Quarterly*, vol. 74, no. 3, Spring 2015, pp. 146–149.

3   For an account of the background to and philosophy for the WA Inc. Royal Commission see Michael Barker, 'Past as Prologue: A Second Anniversary Reflection on the Work of the Royal Commission into WA Inc.' in Mark Brogan and Harry Phillips (eds), *Past as Prologue: The Royal Commission into Commercial Activities of Government and Other Matters*, Edith Cowan University, 1994, pp. 10–19.

4   See Chris Wheeler, 'The public interest: we know it is important but do we know what it means', *AIAL Forum*, vol. 48.

5   Mark Schacter, 'When Accountability Fails: A Framework for Diagnosis and Action', in *ISUMA: Canadian Journal of Public Policy Research*, 2001.

6   Quoted in Sunder Katwala, 'On Reading Bernard Crick', *Open Democracy UK* (23/12/2008).

7   Mark Philp, *The Corruption of Politics*, 2017; warwick.ac.uk/lib-publications.

8   Philp, *The Corruption of Politics*.

9   *Bropho v State of Western Australia*, 2008, FCAFC100.

10   Select Committee on Reserves (Reserve 43131) Bill 2003.

11   See Paige Taylor, 'Land Campaign hid child sex abuse', *The Australian*, 29 February 2008; and Tony Barrass, 'Ugly truth on Bropho', *Perth Now*, 28 October 2011.

12   See Philp, *The Corruption of Politics*.

13   This being said it remains the case, as Peter Drucker observed, that working in an organisation 'the value system of which is unacceptable to a person, or incompatible with it, condemns the person to frustration and non-performance'. We all need to take the mirror test; 'What kind of person do I want to see?' See his *Management Challenges for the 21st Century*, Harper Business, 1999, pp. 175–178.

14   Peter Aucoin, 'New Public Governance in Westminster Systems: Impartial Public Administration and Management Performance at Risk', *Governance: An International Journal of Policy, Administration and Institutions*, vol. 25, no. 2, April 2012, p. 179.

15   'The Study of Administration', *Political Science Quarterly*, vol. 2, June 1887, p. 201.

16   UK Cabinet Office, *Strategy Survival Guide*, Prime Minister's Strategy Unit, July 2004, pp. 9–10.

17   See Geoff Gallop, 'Putting the public back into the public service' in *Politics, Society, Self: occasional writings*, UWA Publishing, 2012.

18   On the case for proper regulation, see *Second Report of the WA Inc. Royal Commission*, 1992, p. 6.4.

19   For my own view on rights and corruption and their link to government, see 'The Case for a Charter of Rights', *University of Notre Dame Australia Law Review*, vol. 12, December 2010, pp. 33–44; and, 'The Accountability Debate in Canberra: What's at Stake?' *The Mandarin*, 17 April 2019.

CHAPTER 6

Maintaining public trust in government

Peter Shergold

Dream on: the creation of public value without a public service

Reflecting on Tom Frame's chapter in this collection on the place of universities in Australian national life, I was moved to a provocative thought. It was an idea so shocking that perhaps I should not dare to speak its name. Frame relays a perceptive question that was posed by Simon Marginson, Professor of Higher Education at the University of Melbourne: namely, 'what greater good would be lost if universities closed tomorrow?'[1] This led me quietly to muse, 'what public benefit would disappear if the institutional structure of public services were to collapse?'

I have spent three decades working as a senior public servant, drafting government reports, speaking at conferences and writing articles on public policy. I have thought long and hard about how to improve the organisational effectiveness of the agencies of public administration. But, in truth, I had never considered the matter in such stark terms before.

Would the loss of a professional class of public officials really diminish faith in the exercise of democratic governance? Alternatively, is it possible that the competitive provision of more customer-centric public services by business or civil society organisations might actually improve the confidence of citizens in the efficacy of government? Perhaps the abolition of public services as separate institutions might encourage the private and not-for-profit sectors to step in and enhance the efficiency, effectiveness and capability of program design and delivery. Perhaps their very absence might lead to greater innovation and entrepreneurial energy directed to the creation of public value. Perhaps the marketisation of public service implementation (the provision of order and security, the collection of revenues and the payment of benefits) might drive better practice. Why not replace so-called 'New Public Management' with no agencies of public management at all?

This wholesale promulgation of an untrammelled neo-liberal agenda should not too quickly be dismissed simply as ideological pie in the sky, bye and bye. After all, Australian public administration has moved significantly in this direction in the last generation, across all jurisdictions. Most publicly-funded community services are now put out to tender and delivered under contract by outsourced providers. More broadly, many public services, whilst extensively regulated by governments, are now delivered by non-government bodies – think child care, education and training, health services and aged care. Meanwhile, public infrastructure is increasingly designed, built and/ or operated through forms of public-private-partnership.

In the 1990s, there was much talk in Coalition ranks about introducing what Americans called the 'Yellow Pages Test'. At its most simple, the proposition was that if a government activity could be undertaken by a commercial company listed in the telephone directory, then the activity should be market-tested, benchmarked against private sector performance and, if the private operator was more competitive, contracted out. This philosophy underpinned the abolition of the Commonwealth Employment Service and the introduction of the competitive Job Network in 1996 – although, as it turned out, community for-purpose organisations succeeded in winning just as large a share of the business from public sector providers as did their private for-profit rivals.

Why not now be more radical still and allow governments, under legislative scrutiny, to simply buy in their policy advice and program delivery expertise, scrapping the idea of a large permanent administration? Why not redesign the 'Yellow Pages Test' for a digital era, in which global connectivity has the potential to harness public policy skills from all sorts of experts around the world in real time? As we deploy the cognitive technology of the 'Fourth Industrial Revolution', perhaps the institutional structures born of the First Industrial Revolution have passed their use-by date?

Already, ever-increasing levels of government expenditure are directed outside the public services in order to access avowedly superior expertise amongst consultancy companies. By 2017 the Commonwealth Government's annual spend on consultants had risen to around $4.6 billion.[2] States and territories are following suit. Meanwhile, law firms scrap and scramble to get placed on the legal panels which allow them to win lucrative government work. As a consequence, the private sector is winning ever larger contracts to provide governments with the policy advice that was in times gone by the exclusive domain of public servants.

Moreover, within the structures of government, power relations have already shifted in significant ways. Since the State and Commonwealth governments of Don Dunstan (South Australia, 1970–79) and Gough Whitlam (Canberra, 1972–75), politically-aligned advisers have been appointed to provide alternative sources of policy advice to the ministers who employ them. These 'staffers' are seen as friends to governments, sharing their political agenda. Unsurprisingly, ministers often trust them more than career bureaucrats, with their avowed ethos of impartiality.

In all jurisdictions, staffers have become more influential. The number of Commonwealth ministerial advisers has risen sharply from 155 in 1972 to 423 in 2015.[3] The job now provides a stepping stone to elected office: by 2016, 49 percent of Liberal members and senators and 55 percent of Labor members and senators in the Federal Parliament had previously been employed as staffers, electorate officers or advisers.[4] Why not now be bolder and, in a nod to the American system, accept that an incoming Australian government can select far more of its senior executives from outside public service ranks?

Pragmatic concerns about the economic costs of such democratic disruption every few elections might easily be alleviated. We could, for example, provide greater political stability by moving to fixed five-year terms and ensuring that contracts were staggered and extended beyond the electoral cycle. A Parliamentary Office of Procurement, sitting alongside the Auditor-General and Ombudsman, could ensure that due processes were followed and the potential for corrupt practices minimised. In such a world, Oppositions would operate far more as shadow governments, always ready to take power. We would likely see the emergence in Australia of well-staffed, well-funded, politically-aligned think tanks (perhaps publically supported) and an 'administration-in-exile' comprised of business executives, unionists, community leaders and academics.

Here is the rather disturbing truth: a cursory perusal of my recent writing on public service matters might suggest that I would be broadly supportive of such a transformation in organising the delivery of public value. Certainly, I have recommended that public services become far more open institutions, with more flexible and agile structures. I have suggested that the culture of public service needs to be more outward-looking. And I have not stopped there. I have routinely portrayed the outsourcing of public service delivery as a revolution half-fulfilled. Rather than simply contracting organisa-tions to deliver public programs on their behalf, governments could do far more to involve third-party providers in the design of the programs. I have 'walked the talk', doing my best to involve non-government organisations in collaborative partnerships and joint working groups. I have supported human-centred design processes in which those citizens who will receive a form of government support are given an opportunity to contribute to its development. Such initiatives can broaden and deepen the creation of public value in ways that actively engage the 'citizenry'. I am all for it.[5]

Hold fast : the increasing value of public service traditions

It is a thought-provoking exercise to imagine that the directions of public service in recent decades could end up with no institutional public service at all. And yet, in spite of my unmistakeable enthusiasm for a more modern and adaptive form of twenty-first century governance, I am not attracted by my reverie.

At heart, I remain a traditionalist. Indeed, I have become increasingly con-vinced that a formal public service, rooted firmly in mid-nineteenth century values, is a vital institutional element of public trust. In my considered view, the maintenance of a democratic and civil society depends upon it. A profes-sional and apolitical cadre of public administrators, committed to serving and advising successive governments with equal impartiality, is a cornerstone of a liberal democracy. In its way it is just as important as representative and responsible government, independent judicial review and the scrutiny of a free press. The stewardship of public assets for future generations is a responsibility that should rest firmly on the shoulders of public servants.

More than ever the survival of the 'public service' will best serve the interests of the Australian public. I say 'more than ever' advisedly. Thirty years ago I was cautiously optimistic that Francis Fukuyama had it right in proclaiming the 'end of history' in the sense that liberal democracies had emerged as the final form of human governance.[6] No longer. The depressing fact is that here, as elsewhere, trust in democracy appears to be falling. There is plenty of evidence that politicians are now trusted only by a small minority of the public. Other traditional bastions of society – church ministers, business executives, union leaders and lawyers – are less respected than in the past. Suspicion of expertise is increasing, conspiracy theories run rampant even amongst more educated people and, partly in consequence, the appeal of populism seems to be growing apace. Citizen expectations are increasing faster than the capacity of governments to deliver.[7]

Authoritarianism has re-emerged as the greatest threat to liberal democratic values. The 'strongmen' are striking back, offering autocratic certainty to disillusioned citizens, particularly to people who find themselves disheartened by the perceived mismanagement, incompetence and corruption of democratic decision-making.[8] In the 'post-truth' era of social media, people have come to curate the news to fit their existing perceptions (or, unwittingly, have clever algorithms do it for them). They too rarely read, listen or talk to others of a different political opinion. Particularly online, civil discourse and political debate has become ever less civil. I worry that the democratic centre does not seem to be holding against the forces of identity-based political tribalism.

In such a world, marked by increasing fragmentation and division, it seems to me that a non-partisan public service is more vital than ever. Trained to assess the merits and risks of all sides of a political argument, it can bring a voice of moderated civility to democratic decision-making. It is able to negotiate the iterative processes of political compromise. Evidence and experience can be brought to bear on the wickedly complex conundrums of public policy. The vocation of public service can help governments to govern: equally, it can help to ensure public accountability for how they govern. By its presence, a professional public service acts as a bulwark against the exercise of untrammelled executive authority. It is worth preserving.

Change up : improving how the public service works

But not just as it is. If public services continue to do the same old things in much the same old way, they will continue to reinforce the view that democracy really does not work very well. It can seem too cumbersome, too unwieldy, too slow. In Charles Dickens' wonderful imagination it an be a modern variant of 'The Circumlocution of Office'. The question, is how can the traditional structures, systems and culture of institutional public service be made fit for the purpose of restoring faith in democratic processes?

The contributors to this volume, drawing on our particular perspectives, seek to set out the ways in which public trust in government can be enhanced. We have been challenged to identify practical ways in which to improve the public interest. From the viewpoint of a senior public servant mandarin, one step removed, I suggest that there are five matters that need to be addressed. None speaks the exciting language of 'innovation'. Indeed, my proposals are rather modest. They focus not on improving the efficiency, effectiveness, capability and productivity of public services – important though those matters are – but, instead, on how they might build more effective relation-ships within the political and civic structures that frame the articulation of public purpose. Taken together, they have the capacity to help restore faith in democratic governance.

Enhancing the status of government delivery

Prime Minister Scott Morrison is not the first head of the executive branch of government (the President of the Senate and the Speaker of the House of Representatives are heads of the legislative branch) to emphasise that the most important thing that he wants to see 'is some congestion-busting in the bureaucracy, ensuring that we get things done'. His is a simple proposition: the Australian Public Service (APS) needs to deliver government programs on time, on budget, to public expectations.[9] Yet senior public servants themselves, at least in their private conversations, will be concerned that the Prime Minister's remarks seem to ascribe too narrow an ambit to their expertise. Their perceived role, first and foremost, is to make sure that the policy frameworks that support government services and programs are properly designed and costed.

I often sense that there still exists an unstated perception in the senior ranks of public services that there are 'A' and 'B' leadership teams, demarcated between those with the analytical and conceptual skills to design policies and those of more modest talent who can oversee the delivery of the programs that give them effect. When I was asked to examine the tragic failure of the rollout of the Home Insulation Program which had been introduced by the Rudd Government in 2009, it was starkly apparent that it foundered on hopelessly inadequate risk mitigation and project management.[10] Such vital skills were simply not accorded the importance that they should have been. That status bias still prevails in too many government agencies, although there are encouraging signs that things are beginning to change.

In fact, the distinction sometimes drawn between the design and delivery of policy – between the administrative 'centre' and the organisational 'line' – is entirely misconceived. The public can only judge the success of a government policy by the manner in which it is implemented, not by how elegant it might have appeared on paper. No matter how well conceived any new public program, there will still need to be learning by doing in its delivery. That is why governments should be far more willing to trial and demonstrate new approaches to service delivery, building in continuing evaluation and adapting and improving processes prior to a more extensive scaling-up. This may scarcely appear to be a perceptive insight, yet governments and their public servants are too rarely willing to experiment before they roll-out new initiatives. As a consequence, citizens too often find themselves having to access government programs in which substantial 'teething problems' are still evident. Public trust is undermined.

Opening up the borders of public service

One of the most important characteristics of Australian public services, that can be traced back to the British *Northcote-Trevelyan Report* of 1854, is that their hierarchical structures should be built on recognition of individual merit rather than on nepotism or patronage. Of course, definitions of merit have widened over time. Seniority, once regarded as a good proxy for learned experience, is now accorded far less relevance as a means of assessing ability, capacity and drive. Moreover, the careful processes of appointment and promotion that prevail in most public agencies now recognise that there is value in recruiting and developing a broad spectrum of talent across lines of gender and ethnicity: it is a matter of enhancing productive diversity not just meeting an 'access and equity' requirement. This is especially true to the extent that bureaucratic structures are now much flatter than in the past and team-based approaches to work more common.

Yet, too often, the veneer of due process in selecting the 'best' candidates for public service jobs continues to privilege those who are already inside the sector, over external candidates. In part that explains why mobility in and out of public services, especially at senior levels, remains unduly restricted. Potential, rather than insider experience, needs to be accorded much greater value in gauging merit. Borders need to be made far more porous. While there will always be a place for career public servants, it needs to be made much easier for individuals to move in, out and back to the public sector. The broader experience and expertise of 'outsiders' can be harnessed to particular public policy initiatives. Mobility needs to be actively encouraged between agencies and across sectors. A truly open public service is likely to be far more innovative, adaptive and responsive to the government it serves.

Provocatively, I can imagine large parts of the public service as 'flash organisations', with external experts recruited across sectors to work together for short periods as project-oriented teams. I can see advantages in the 'Hollywood Model' of work in which people with different skill sets and experiences come together to get a job done and then disperse again. It seems to me ideally suited to many public service projects.

Speaking (and writing) truth to political power

It is an important truth – albeit one that has become a rather tired cliché – that impartial public servants should provide 'frank and fearless' advice to the ministers that they serve. Of course, it needs to be properly understood that, at the end of even the most protracted and robust discussion between ministers and public servants, it is the democratically elected government of the day that should make the final decisions, not technically expert administrators, however gifted.

When I was Secretary of the Department of the Prime Minister and Cabinet (PM&C), inducting groups of newcomers each month, they often asked at what stage I would stop trying to push for an outcome that the government resisted. When, in the words of Sir William Cole, would the prosecution of my arguments become nagging? My answer was that, in policy arguments, I would always say 'yes' at the point at which I was persuaded that the decision was being made by ministers whose eyes were wide open. I needed to have concluded they had considered all alternative options, were fully aware of potentially unintended consequences and had properly understood the financial and organisational risks attached to implementation.

It is sometimes asserted in the media that today's public service 'mandarins' have become wimps and no longer possess the steadfastness of their predecessors in challenging ministerial viewpoints. It is suggested that in part this is because secretaries and directors-general have lost the comforting privilege of the permanent status that they once enjoyed. On the basis of my own experience, I am unpersuaded by that argument: the avowed 'courage' required to present views to a minister that they might prefer not to hear seems to me a matter of character rather than of contract. I never found it a very intimidating proposition. The ministers that I have served – from Robert Tickner on the political left to Peter Reith on the political right – never I think doubted my willingness to argue a case. Equally, they always understood that, when the government decision was made, I would strive my best to implement it with commitment (and took quiet pride in the fact that through my actions no-one, outside a small inner circle, would ever know whether I had argued for or against the policy I was delivering). John Howard, reflecting on his time as prime minister (1996–2007), acknowledged the widespread nostalgia for the outstanding public servants of the past but indicated that he found it hard to accept that his departmental secretaries – Max Moore-Wilton and myself – were inherently less effective or professional than the best of their predecessors.[11] I hope he was correct.

I do not wish to appear complacent. There are worrying signs. I am particularly concerned that the introduction and progressive widening of Freedom of Information (FOI) legislation, designed with the best of intentions to protect the public interest, may be having precisely the opposite effect to what was anticipated.

Ministers today often prefer to have public service views on sensitive issues presented orally for fear that any written advice may be sought under FOI and become public. The danger is that such oral communication is less well-argued, not fully understood and can be plausibly denied in the future by one or both of the interlocutors. It is my strong opinion that frank advice on a complex issue needs to be conveyed in a written brief. It can nearly always be clearer and its arguments not lost in the unintentional ambiguities of the spoken word. With the best (or worst) of motives, people remember conversations differently.

It would be far better if a small class of documents – those designed for the deliberative purposes of guiding government decision-making – were to be exempted from the public scrutiny of FOI legislation. There is a public interest benefit in public servants and ministers being mutually assured that their policy discussions remain confidential. The breaking of confidentiality, either as a result of legislation or leaking, probably does more to erode trust and respect between ministers and public servants than any other cause. It undermines the creation of good policy. That is scarcely in the public interest. After all, in most circumstances a government should be held to public account for what it decides to do, rather than for the public service advice that it decides to reject.[12]

Sharing space where public policy is made

Public servants no longer have the same monopoly access to the ear of their ministers that prevailed in generations past. That is a good thing. There is considerable value in senior public servants having to argue their case in the marketplace of competing political ideas. Ministers can now seek views from their staffers, professional consultants and public think-tanks. Lobbyists and advocates will seek to win them over. The 'mandarin' has but one voice in the raucous cacophony of competing advice.

In truth, however, it remains a persuasive voice. Well-trained public servants remain well-positioned to play a vital role in providing advice to ministers. Ideally they should not seek peremptorily to close down debate or attempt to limit the options being brought forward for consideration. Rather they should aim to facilitate broad engagement between the minister and those many others who wish to exert influence. Senior public servants still have a central position in the organisational structure of decision-making. They retain situational authority, enabling their minister to direct the rather opaque and ambiguous processes by which policies are drafted, negotiated, amended and compromised. They will often have much better access than others to the private meetings and intergovernmental committees at which policy proposals are finalised for Cabinet discussion. Their skill lies in overseeing the iterative dynamics by which public policy is shaped.

The challenge is to ensure that all the players, some of whom may have been contracted by public servants to provide a report to their ministers, remain aware of their particular roles in the process and properly understand how to conduct their relationships. This injunction applies most particularly to ministerial advisers, given their power to convey directions to public servants on behalf of their ministers.

Let me be clear: unlike many observers of contemporary politics, I believe that the advisers in ministerial offices perform a valuable role. They ensure that ministers (and shadow ministers) can be advised by people who share their party affiliation or political ideology. Their presence in the system makes it easier for public servants to focus their attention on apolitical advice. They add to the diversity of skills, experience, perspectives and ideas available to support decision-making. The brazenness of their partiality can be a useful balance to the considered impartiality and caution of public servants.

Tensions arise when the advisers over-reach. The ever-present danger is that they may choose to use their gate-keeping position to block the advice of public servants with whom they disagree or – worse – leave public servants unclear whether or not ministers have seen the arguments drafted for their consideration. At all times, a minister needs to be clear on what advice has been provided by the department and to have at least taken into account the propositions put forward. Of course, it remains a matter for the minister to decide which direction to take.

My successor as Secretary of the Department of the Prime Minister and Cabinet, Terry Moran, came to the disheartening conclusion that advisers were 'becoming a black hole of accountability within our parliamentary democracy.'[13] I understand his angst. Many advisers do not sufficiently comprehend that the significant power they wield is derived from their minister's executive authority and that they should be held accountable for their actions to parliament through their minister. They need to recognise that only with the explicit agreement of their ministers do they have the right to instigate policy formulation by public servants, to comment upon it, but never to reject it on their minister's behalf. They do not possess the power to direct public servants, to change their advice where it differs from their own view, or to 'protect' ministers from seeing proposals with which they disagree.

There can be no doubt that many public servants are uncomfortable with the manner in which some advisers presently seek to wield their derived powers. A survey that I undertook on behalf of the Institute of Public Administration Australia (IPAA) in 2018 suggested that 58 percent of state public servants, and 62 percent of Commonwealth public servants, thought that ministerial advisers played too big a role.[14] That finding should ring alarm bells. At the very least, in the political space where public policy is decided, advisers need to be subject to administrative or legislative guidelines that explicitly set out the limits of their power.

Enhancing collaboration, within and without

My former colleague and departmental secretary, Roger Beale, opined in his valedictory speech in 2004, 'that those great men of the post-war public service were also great haters and great players of time-wasting, self-indulgent bureaucratic games. Inter-departmental warfare was rife and personal feuds carried out over decades abounded.'[15] His view, with which I heartily concur, was that contemporary public servants have become more inclined to take a whole-of-government view of issues rather than a narrowly departmental one. In today's public services, there is a greater sense of the value of collaboration in overcoming bureaucratic demarcations.

Turf protection is just as likely to come from ministers as from the bureaucrats who support them. Yet few of the significant issues that face government today fit neatly within the functional silos created for administrative convenience. Most policies need to be informed by a wide range of official expertise, both from central and line agencies. That is why effective Cabinet processes are so often a good indicator of effective governance. It is not just that important matters should be subject to collective discussion by ministers but that public servants, to enhance that process, should be required to circulate their departmental policy proposals to other agencies for comment, criticism or support. When these processes are short-circuited, the design and delivery of public policy is nearly always weakened. In my experience, proposals that are accepted into Cabinet 'under the line' on the basis of perceived urgency are nearly always inadequately prepared. In general, neither the full costs nor the risks of such proposals are adequately recognised.

While accepting that cross-agency collaboration is necessary, it can no longer be regarded as sufficient. For public servants to design a program for government and then, most usually, tender it out for delivery represents a hopelessly inadequate way of developing evidence-based policy. Mechanisms need to be found to ensure that first-hand experience (whether of community providers or frontline public servants) can be incorporated into the design of the programs that they will end up delivering. I have discovered that simple mistakes and wrong assumptions could often have been avoided if providers' views had been heard earlier. Risks can be identified and mitigated. Outcomes can be improved.

It needs to be borne in mind that the perspective of community organisations or social enterprises often mediates the experience of the clients that they serve (and on behalf of whom they often advocate). Public policy is better still if it can capture directly the authentic lived experience of those who are the target of its programs and services. Today there is much talk of 'human-centred design' but too rarely is that methodology extended to include the perspectives of those who will be benefitted or regulated. As a consequence, behavioural insights, so crucial to effective public policy, are often lost. People – the 'public' – often behave and respond to government initiatives in perplexingly 'irrational' ways: so much better then to find them out in advance.

Moreover, government (and their public servants) should be more willing to design programs that are not just rolled out across a federal or state jurisdiction. Programs can be trialed. New approaches can be piloted. Success can be demonstrated, problems alleviated, early failures learned from. Public servants are now learning the value of being able to modify and tailor programs to particular communities of place or identity. Programs can be designed to empower 'consumers' to exert control and direction over delivery in ways which best meet their needs. The more that citizens can feel they are active players in public policy, the greater will be their faith and commitment to democratic governance.

✻ ✻ ✻ ✻

The proposals I have made can be achieved through relatively modest changes to the institutional structures, legislative framework and workplace systems of public services and parliamentary government. In that narrow sense, little is required to improve public trust within the 'political' environment and, more significantly, between public administrators and the wider community.

Far more challenging, however, my suggestions require a profound change in mindset. They necessitate a transformation in cultural expectations. Governments, through their ministers, need to provide explicit authority and encouragement for their public servants to offer untrammelled policy advice and to manage (rather than avoid) the risks attached to experimentation in the design and delivery of programs and services. Equally, public servants should feel confident that it is governments which exercise executive power to make decisions. Appropriately, governments should hold their officials to account for the implementation of their policy decisions.

Public servants need to recognise that they are responsible for the effective actioning of policies, if not for their results and consequences. For their part, ministerial advisers should accept accountability for the important role they play as 'go-betweens'. Actions should be transparent. All sides need formal training in properly understanding the respective powers that they exercise: only on such a basis can mutual understanding and trust be built.

Public servants also need to learn to use their situational power not to control and limit alternative viewpoints but, instead, to guide the capacity of the private, community and academic sectors to contribute evidence, experience and ideas to governments. They need to be navigators rather than gatekeepers. They need to exercise facilitative leadership. They need to manage cross-sectoral relationships, not contracts. Their ambition should not just be to improve 'customer service' and enable 'consumer-directed care' but to help citizens find a path through the complexities of government processes and provide more opportunities for them to participate in democracy in a continuing manner.

In effect, public servants need to envisage themselves as agents of governance. In this deep sense they are stewards of the systems which create and maintain public value. In effect, they should stand as guardians of the public interest and take pride in their role in maintaining public trust in democratic purpose. It all sounds rather grand. Indeed it is, but is also a realisable ambition. It couches the traditional values of public service, and articulates workplace culture, in contemporary terms. You may say that I am a dreamer, but I'm certainly not the only one. Imagine … it is easy if you try.

Endnotes

1   Simon Marginson, 'The modern university must reinvent itself to survive,' *The Conversation,* 11 March 2011. Available at www.theconversation.com>.

2   'Federal Government underestimated consulting spend by billions'. Available at www. consultancy.com.au>, 26 February 2018.

3   Yee-Fui Ng, 'Between law and convention : ministerial advisers in the Australian system of responsible government,' paper presented to the Senate occasional lecture series at Parliament House, 21 July 2017, p. 115. Available at www.researchgate.net>.

4   Tom McIlroy, 'Australia's career political class : rising numbers of Australian MPs are former staffers and ministerial advisers,' *Sydney Morning Herald*, updated 25 March 2017. Available at www.smh.com.au>.

5   See, for example, Peter Shergold, 'Re-imagining public service,' *Australian Journal of Social Sciences,* Vol.52, 2017. 4–12; 'Creating public innovation through collabora-tion : government, business and the social services sector' in We Wei Neng (ed.), *Adaptive Governance in a Changing World*, 2016, 151–164; and 'Three sectors : one public purpose' in John R Butcher and David Gilchrist (eds), *The Three Sector Solution : Delivering Public Policy in Collaboration with Not-for-Profits and Business*, 2016, pp. 23–32.

6   Francis Fukuyama, 'The end of history?' *The National Interest,* Summer 1989, 1–18. For Fukiyama's own more recent doubts see Louis Menand, 'Francis Fukuyama postpones the end of history,' *The New Yorker*, 27 August 2018. Available at www.newyorker.com>.

7   The Museum of Australian Democracy annual survey suggests that satisfaction with government in Australia has fallen from 86 percent in 2007 to 41 percent in 2018 : see Gareth Hutchens, 'Australians no longer trust their democracy, survey finds,' *The Guardian*, 4 December 2018. Available at www.theguardian.com.au> . On declining Australian faith in democracy and politicians see Lowy Institute Poll 2019 (which shows only 65 percent of Australians say that 'democracy is preferable to any other kind of government'), available at www.lowyinstitute.org> and Ross Morgan Image of Professions Survey 2917, (which shows trust in Australian Federal and State MP's at only 16 per cent), available at www.thompsonsaustralia.com.au>.

8   Robert Kagan, 'The strongmen strike back', *The Washington Post*, 14 March 2018. Available at www.washingtonpost.com>.

9   Laura Tingle, 'Scott Morrison has the public service and accountability in his sights, but what's behind the rhetoric?' ABC News, 26 July 2019. Available at www.abc.net. au> See also Michelle Gratton, 'Scott Morrison tells public servants keep in mind that "bacon and egg" principle', *The Conversation*, 18 August 2019. Available at www. theconversation.com>.

10   Peter Shergold, *Learning from Failure : Why large government policy initiatives have gone so badly wrong in the past and how the chances of success in the future can be improved*, August 2015, 53–61. Available at www.apsc.gov.au>.

11   John Howard, *The Menzies Era : The Years that Shaped Modern Australia*, 2014, p. 370.

12   These arguments are expanded at Peter Shergold, *Learning from Failure*, pp. 16–24.

13   John Alford, 'Terry Moran: time for an inquiry into the public service', *The Conversation*, 1 November 2012. Available at www.theconversation.com> More recently Moran has characterised the role of ministerial advisers as morphing into something 'quite different and dangerous', see Doug Dingwall, 'Bring ministers' advisors under greater scrutiny ; ex-PM&C chief', *Sydney Morning Herald*, 26 March 2019. Available at www. smh.com.au>.

14   For accounts of this survey see Jessica Irvine, 'The policy chaos eroding our faith in democracy', *Sydney Morning Herald*, 19 November 2018. Available at *www.the-mandarin.com.au*> See also Harley Dennett, 'Crisis of confidence : a black dog stalks the public service', *The Mandarin*, 17 October 2018. Available at www.themandarin. com.au>.

15   Roger Beale, 'Yes, Minister – the privileged position of secretaries', in John Wanna, Sam Vincent and Andrew Podger (eds), *With the Benefit of Hindsight: Valedictory Reflections from Departmental Secretaries, 2004–2011*, 2012, p. 2.

CHAPTER 7

Character and the public interest

John Uhr

I have been invited to clarify the role of 'character' arising from my chapter on the public sector in the previous book in this series, *Who Defines the Public Interest?*[1] A theme of that chapter was that a certain type of 'political character' was required by those in the public sector accepting some sort of official responsibility for acting in the public interest. Two controversial issues arose. First, public officials who believed that their role required them to safeguard 'the public interest' faced something of a test of character. Second, the best solution to this test was a certain type of 'political character' not often acknowledged in public sector studies. Debate easily arises over the place of personal character in public policy and over suggestions that political character is a desirable form of personal character.

These are not small issues. Is it true that personal character or temperament matters in public sector performance? Is it true that political character also matters in public sector performance? This chapter tries to clarify what 'political character' means for those officials managing public interest issues.

My use of the term, 'political character', suggests that the public interest is associated with a certain type of character with surprisingly valuable political qualities. Not all forms of political character fit the role. Think of two extreme forms of political character which surround the right form of political character we are trying to identify. The passive extreme is an idealised form of political impartiality often associated with public sector norms of apolitical neutrality. Officials here would be expected to act with high degrees of political impartiality. The other extreme is much more actively political: officials would be expected to act with zealous partisanship. The politically passive type of character might be admirable in many ways but it can fall short in public interest decision-making. So, too, the active or partisanly political character can over-step the public interest mark.

Somewhere between these two extremes sits the type of political character we want to explore. Both extremes have weak forms of political judgment: the passive types believe that their role is to suppress personal political judgment; and the active types rely only on highly partisan agendas often found in highly politicised styles of public administration with very strong executive governments. My suggestion is that the intermediate character is politically prudent and capable of promoting and leading public judgment about the public interest. I have tried to document this in a book of political theory defending what I call 'prudential public leadership'.[2] My claim is that the public interest is best managed by officials whose political character is shaped around the classic virtue of prudence: the defining quality of personal character according to classical political theorists like Aristotle – whose realism influences much of modern political thought.[3]

Can academics help us understand political character?

We can now start to locate the type of personal character that is political according to this model of prudence. In my chapter in *Who Defines the Public Interest?*, I noted two academics with prominent roles in examining the public interest. One is my former Australian National University colleague and Professor of Public Administration at the London School of Economics, the late Peter Self, who wrote extensively on public interest implications of liberal-democratic civil services. The other is the American public administration scholar, the late Professor Herbert J Storing, who co-authored with Self a book on interest group politics, and many other studies.[4] Both of these scholars wrote extensively on 'bureaucratic statesmanship' by which they meant the public interest responsibilities of senior civil servants – where their 'on the job' character derives from their constitutional oath or role as professional administrators, and not directly from their individual character or personality.

Not mentioned in that chapter is that I was a close professional colleague of one of Storing's most influential students, late American public administration theorist professor John Rohr, whose early book *Ethics for Bureaucrats* examined the public interest implications arising from the professional oath of office required of American civil servants.[5] The link to our discussion is that these three academic authorities (Self, Storing and Rohr) hold that the public interest is reinforced not so much by personal as *official* or *constitutional* character: their term for 'political character'. Official or constitutional character is displayed in officials' prudence or sense of judgment about the best use of their official or constitutional powers. Almost always, prudence is *not* exercised by passive neutrality or active zealotry. Personal character is always relevant but *not* in the simplified senses of remaining passively neutral or actively becoming partisan. Character matters when, in pressing concrete circumstances, prudence helps officials judge how best to protect the public interest.

How does prudence help political character?

The primary theme for this discussion is being 'political'. A conventional model holds that those who get to occupy high positions of public trust are assumed to have the right personal or political character to carry out the job. They bring their character into the job. Even better, they shape the job around their character, stamping their 'personality' on the job. When a new occupant replaces the former occupant, the job is reshaped around the new character with its new 'personality', reflecting a tendency in the management of high public offices to 'let the person drive the job'. In this sense, job performance is a character test, where the occupant brings their personal or political character to the job and defines the job around what they 'characteristically' judge to be their core professional responsibilities.

My 2018 chapter reviewed a number of public office case studies where debates over the public interest emerged. The point to notice is that in all cases, advocates of the public interest defined job character by reference to the job – and not to the qualities of the person wanting to hold the job. In some important sense, the character of the job framed the responsibilities of the character of the job holder. Advocates of the public interest might say that the public responsibilities of office *tested* the private character of office holders: that is, effective job performance depended on occupants 'fitting in' with the expected roles of the office.

The implication might then be that job performance depends, at the very least, on selecting occupants whose personal or political character is consistent with the public character of the office. Persons of character (colourful character, prominent character, commanding character, known character, disarming character or whatever) have to show that, as public and not simply as individual characters, they can perform according to the highest public standards of the office or role or persona. Prudence is the skill or competency that generates this type of political performance.

Are United States presidents good examples of prudential political characters?

The biggest example comes from one of the biggest jobs ever: the office of the President of the United States. Almost every type of personal character has had a chance to be tested for that presidential job. Many types of quite ordinary characters have passed that test and held office as (often quite ordinary) presidents. Of interest to us is professional debate by governance experts over what sort of characters deserve to have the job of the President of the United States. The United States Constitution spells out, in article two in less than two pages, some essentials: executive power (otherwise undefined) is vested in the president, who must be a natural-born citizen aged at least 35 and have been a resident of the United States for 14 years; who takes the constitutional oath of office ('to preserve, protect and defend' – not the United States – but 'the Constitution of the United States'); and may (as may 'all civil officers') be impeached for 'treason, bribery, or other high crimes and misdemeanours'.

Academic scholarship on the United States presidency has a lot to say about the place of character in the top office in the executive branch of government. The American journal, *Presidential Studies Quarterly*, is a convenient point of entry into that area of scholarly debate: see, for example, the special issue of 2010 on the office and the ethics of the presidency.[6]

Two very senior American academics (Dennis Thompson of Harvard and William Galston of the Brookings Institution) have articles about 'constitutional character' which the American constitutional framers expected of holders of this office. The original understanding of the American framers was that the test of office was not the personal excellence (or even the engaging personal vices) of claimants but their excellence as 'constitutional characters' using executive power in a particular constitutional setting. Personal character would be tested by a president's ability to take on the official role as chief executive: that is, 'to play the part' prudently.

This can sound a bit too Machiavellian, as though decent personal character does not really matter. This type of hard-boiled 'realism' certainly dominates Max Weber's influential theory of modern leadership, where the leader does whatever reason of state or strict necessity demands. This model is only half right: it is more about *decisiveness* than prudence. But the American framers took their bearing about the office or role of political character from the founder of liberal constitutionalism, John Locke, whose *Second Treatise of Government*, published in 1689, highlights the role of discretion and prudence in executive government. Locke carefully unwraps 'prerogative power' as the hidden secret of executive leadership, even in liberal systems of representative government.[7] The larger point is that the best way to frame a public official's responsibilities for 'the public interest' is to focus on the institutional office or role to be managed prudently. I have tried to outline one approach to this ethics-of-office framework.[8]

The task now is briefly to review four portraits of public interest prudence canvassed in my 2018 chapter. There is no 'one model' of political character because there is no 'one model' of prudence which varies according to the nature of office or role being performed. My four portraits come from the real world of politics and show how different office-holders in different systems of government can make good prudential judgments to protect the public interest.

Bipartisan political character

Bipartisanship can promote the public interest. Case study one involved Sir Henry Parkes, the longest-serving non-consecutive Premier of the Colony of New South Wales, identifying constitutional principles of responsible government blending public interest determination among ministers, civil servants and, somewhat surprisingly, members of parliament. Parkes' contribution is to show how the political process can share power for determining the public interest across many institutions. Ministers understandably fear leaving this power solely in the hands of bureaucrats; but so too parliaments fear leaving it in the hands solely of ministers. Parkes devised a reform approach to bring more players to the decision table.

Responsive political character

Civil service responsiveness can promote the public interest. Case study two involved Sir Winston Churchill, the former First Lord of the Admiralty and future wartime British prime minister) when deep in opposition in the 1930s, persuading civil servants in high places secretly to hand over official information for Churchill's campaign against appeasement. Two types of role are relevant here. First, Churchill shapes his role as a non-executive backbencher capable of representing core constitutional functions frequently neglected by others in this modest role. Second, many civil servants rethought their official role as responsive administrators when providing confidential government information to an elected member of parliament, Winston Churchill. [Churchill rationalised his access to official information on the grounds that he was a Privy Councillor and also a member of a parliament committee concerned with national defence].

Professional political character

Professionalism within government administration can promote the public interest. Case study three involved Richard Nixon, the 37th President of the United States, 1969–74, confronting official disobedience from many officers in the civil rights division of the Department of Justice. The civil servants rethought their official role as professional lawyers with an *oath of office* to defend the Constitution, including United States Supreme Court directions about desegregation. Their administrative seniors disagreed, preferring the Nixon line to go slow on desegregation.

Civic political character

In liberal democracies, citizens can promote the public interest. Case study four involved Clive Ponting, a Grade 5 (Assistant Secretary) in the United Kingdom Ministry of Defence, who faced court in 1985 after leaking secret government documents on the sinking of the Argentine cruiser, *General Belgrano*, during the 1982 Falklands War. Ponting successfully defended charges brought against him for offences under the *Officials Secrets Act*. Ponting justified his conduct by recovering a constitutional doctrine about parliamentary supremacy. His ministers disagreed. So did the judge at his trial although he was supported by the jury of citizens which exercised its own prudence in acquitting Ponting. The United Kingdom civil service quickly rewrote the line on civil service ethics to thwart future 'Pontings'. Thereafter, the 'public interest' was considered whatever the government of the day said it was.

Conclusion

Character certainly matters in office-holding. A core part of personal character is cultivation and use of the virtue of prudence. This virtue or personal skill is central to the type of political role officials might want to perform. Prudence can be cramped if officials restrict their politics to strict lines of value neutrality; and it can be overtaken if officials opt for the easy solution of zealous partisanship. The public interest is best protected when officials use their personal prudence to judge the proper use of their power according to the concrete and particular circumstances facing them. The four case studies from my 2018 chapter reveal how different those uses of personal power can be in modern democratic systems of government.

Endnotes

1   John Uhr, 'The Public Interest and Public Sector Priorities', in Tom Frame (ed.), *Who Defines the Public Interest?*, Connor Court Publishing, Brisbane, 2018, pp. 114–129.
2   John Uhr, *Prudential Public Leadership: Promoting Ethics in Public Policy and Administration*, Palgrave Macmillan, New York, 2015.
3   Uhr, *Prudential Public Leadership*, pp. 125–146.
4   Uhr, 'The Public Interest and Public Sector Priorities', pp. 125–127.
5   John Rohr, *Ethics for Bureaucrats: An Essay on Law and Values*, foreword by Herbert J Storing, Marcel Dekker, New York, 1978.
6   *Presidential Studies Quarterly*, vol. 40, no. 1, March 2010.
7   John Locke, *Second Treatise*, chapter 14. The entire documents is available at: https://www.earlymoderntexts.com/assets/pdfs/locke1689a.pdf.
8   Uhr, *Prudential Public Leadership*, pp. 178–187.

CHAPTER 8

Excluding the public from the public interest

Clinton Fernandes

T his chapter explains the use of Public Interest Certificates to prevent the public from gaining access to certain government records. It draws on several years of legal proceedings to declassify records on Australia's external relations.

The *Archives Act 1983* provides for a National Archives of Australia, a principal function of which is to preserve and make publicly available the archival resources of the Commonwealth. Concomitant with that function, most records enter an 'open access' period 20 years after they were created. Some records such as Cabinet Notebooks enter the open access period 30 years after they were created, while Census data enters the open access period 99 years after it was created. Once a record enters the open access period, the National Archives must make the record available for public access.

There are several caveats, however, to the public's entitlement to see certain records. For reasons of space, I shall outline only two. A record that has entered the open access period remains an 'exempt record' if its disclosure 'could reasonably be expected to cause damage to the security, defence or international relations of the Commonwealth' or 'was communicated in confidence' by a foreign entity that wishes to maintain the confidentiality of that communication.[1] An 'exempt record' will not be made available to the public.

Declassification of records on Australia's external relations

I have sought the declassification of records relating to Australia's external relations since 2007.[2] The scope of these records has centred around Australia's relations with Indonesia during the Indonesian occupation of East Timor (now Timor-Leste) from 1975–1999. Neither the Department of Foreign Affairs and Trade nor the Department of Defence has a policy of examining records with a view to declassifying them once they enter the open period. Members of the public can request declassification by using the 'Record Search' page of the National Archives website, read the titles of some of its records, and then submit an access request to have them examined for possible declassification. Records whose titles are classified cannot be seen in this 'Record Search' page; people seeking them are required to make a more general request.

I wanted access to records relating to East Timor created by the Defence Intelligence Organisation (DIO) and its predecessors, such as the Joint Intelligence Organisation (JIO). Unable to see any such documents in the Record Search page, I requested access to 'Daily Intelligence Briefs from 1–27 October 1975' and 'Weekly Intelligence Summaries from 1–27 October 1975.' The *Archives Act* provides for a consideration period of 90 business days to allow the National Archives to consult with the relevant Commonwealth Department and make a decision on my application. This consideration period can be extended by mutual agreement – a course of action requested by the National Archives to which I consented. After a series of extensions that lasted more than two years, I used a different provision in the Act to speed things up: the Archives can be 'deemed to have made' a decision refusing access once the consideration period has ended.[3] I decided to use that provision and applied to the Administrative Appeals Tribunal (AAT) for a review of the Archives' decision (deemed, by virtue of the long delay, to have been made to refuse access to the records sought).

The records in question

Once the Administrative Appeals Tribunal entered the picture, the National Archives advised that it had 42 records that were relevant to my application. It claimed, however, that significant portions were deemed 'exempt records' for the reasons specified above. I assessed that the 42 records in question were probably based on intercepts of electronic communications by the Defence Signals Directorate (DSD). A number of books and reports have examined the period in question.[4] I believed much more needed to be written and ony with the official records would that be possible.

This area of research has always been controversial. The reasons can be briefly outlined. In September 1974, the Prime Minister of Australia, Gough Whitlam, met Indonesian President Suharto in Yogyakarta. Whitlam told Suharto that with the imminent end of Portuguese colonial rule, he believed that Indonesia should annex East Timor while paying lip-service to the rights of the East Timorese people to self-determination. In the words of a senior Australian diplomat, 'obeisance has to be made to self-determination.'[5] Accordingly, the Indonesian military devised plans to invade the territory. By October 1975, a terror and destabilisation campaign was underway in the border regions of East Timor. The Indonesian military wanted to seize and hold small enclaves just inside East Timor in order to demoralise the East Timorese and induce them to capitulate.

The Indonesian Government claimed in public that it had no involvement in East Timor. Privately, Indonesian strategists gave detailed advance warning of their military operations to the Australian Embassy. Having accepted these secret briefings without protest – rather, with considerable pride in being let in on the plans – it was in no position to make any public expressions of criticism. As a senior Foreign Affairs official in Canberra warned, 'the Indonesians have, shrewdly, compromised us by making sure that we know their plans for covert intervention in some detail.'[6]

The Embassy's actions elbowed out the prospect of alternatives to Indonesian military action. And there were several viable alternatives. Australia could have lobbied for an internationally supervised referendum on independence. It could also have called for a decolonisation process under United Nations auspices – a process that would have thwarted the Indonesian invasion by internationalising the issue. It could have recognised the indigenous East Timorese political parties, and insisted on their inclusion as representatives of the East Timorese in any decolonisation process. Australia could also have informed its allies in the United Nations Security Council that it wanted an independent East Timor, even if the new country was under heavy Australian influence. It could have convinced East Timor to enter into a treaty relationship with Indonesia, thus assuaging Indonesian concerns and creating a new field for Australia–Indonesia cooperation. None of these alternatives was pursued let alone seriously canvassed.[7]

As Indonesia's terror and destabilisation campaign heightened in October 1975, five foreign journalists (two Australian, two British and one New Zealander) visited the East Timorese village of Balibo, located about ten kilometres from the border with Indonesia. If they had obtained film footage of Indonesia's military campaign and conveyed it to the outside world, Jakarta's cover story would have been blown. Indonesian special forces captured and killed the journalists on the morning of 16 October. They then dressed the corpses in military uniforms, placed guns beside them, and took photographs to portray them as legitimate targets for military action. Concerned about a possible negative reaction internationally, the Indonesian high command called a halt to the military operation. Its logistical difficulties and the onset of the wet season also contributed to this operational pause. There were nearly five weeks of inactivity while the Indonesian leadership waited to assess the international fallout.[8] But there was none. Neither Australia nor Britain nor New Zealand pressed Indonesia at the United Nations on its conduct towards the former Portguese colony. The Indonesian military took this non-reaction as a 'green light'; the lack of international condemnation for killing five foreign journalists was taken to mean it could treat the East Timorese as they wished. That is precisely what Indonesia did. East Timor suffered a death toll amounting to 31 per cent of the population – perhaps the largest loss of life relative to the total population since the Holocaust.[9]

The 42 records identified by the National Archives were about 35 years old at the time of my application to the AAT – well within the open period. It might be supposed that matters pertaining to Australia's diplomatic history, mass atrocities in a neighbouring country, and the unlawful killings of Australian citizens was in the public interest. But the term, the 'public interest', would soon be used in a very different manner.

Public Interest Certificate

The National Archives formally requested that the Attorney-General issue a Public Interest Certificate in the matter. This is an instrument under the *Administrative Appeals Tribunal Act* 1975 requiring the Tribunal to exclude the applicant (me, in this case) from the proceedings while the National Archives and the relevant intelligence agency explained privately to the AAT members their reasons for opposing declassification of the records on the grounds that they should continue to be treated as 'exempt records'. A Public Interest Certificate is self-executing when issued. The AAT has no choice but to hold a secret hearing with only the National Archives and the responsible security agency present.[10]

There are strong public interest reasons why such a certificate should not be issued. First, the records relate to pivotal events in Australian and regional history. There is usually a clear public interest in having such matters, particularly when they are controversial and relate to the lives of ordinary people, ventilated in the interests of democratic debate.

Second, the effect of the certificate requires applicants to reply to assertions they can neither see nor test for accuracy or reasonableness. Applicants are not even entitled to know why the the assertions made for exempting official records from public access are kept from them. It is difficult to imagine a more serious breach of the ordinary principles of natural justice.

Third, the basic principles of open and accountable public administration allow government information be classified only when there is a legitimate reason. When a Public Interest Certificate is issued, the public will never know whether a legitimate reason for the non-disclosure of the material ever existed.

Fourth, there is an obvious public interest in preventing elected and appointed officials from hiding behind Public Interest Certificates to avoid any scrutiny of their decisions and actions. The public interest is much better served by having the legitimacy of any claim for non-disclosure tested under cross-examination.

Fifth, the documents I am seeking relate to events occurring more than four decades ago. East Timor has been an independent sovereign state since 2002. The principal Indonesian political and military figures associated with alleged war crimes and crimes against humanity before and after the invasion are dead and beyond prosecution. Indonesia has experienced major political change since 1975. Any damage to Australia's current relations with Indonesia is, therefore, unlikely.

Notwithstanding these compelling considerations, the Attorney-General issued a Public Interest Certificate as requested by the National Archives on the grounds that disclosure of the information 'would be contrary to the public interest because it would prejudice the security, defence or international relations of Australia'.[11] The Certificate severely limited the ability of the applicant – in this case, me – to test any of the claims being made.

Meanwhile, the United States – Australia's closest military ally and partner in intelligence collection and sharing – has extensively declassified information and documents relating to signals intelligence activities dating from the same era. The National Security Agency, which is the United States' counterpart to Australia's Defence Signals Directorate, has released signals intelligence material relating to the Korean War (1950–53), the Cuban Missile Crisis (1962) and the Vietnam War (1962–75).[12] These events are no less potentially controversial than the Indonesian invasion of East Timor. Clearly, a different understanding of the public interest prevails in the United States.

A proliferation of Public Interest Certificates

Subsequent Attorneys-General have issued Public Interest Certificates in a number of applications for access to archival records. For example, applications have been made before the Administrative Appeals Tribunal for records generated by the Australian Secret Intelligence Service (ASIS) relating to Cambodia in 1969. These papers, now 50 years old, illustrate an important point that should not be overlooked.

It has been credibly reported that ASIS operated on behalf of the United States Central Intelligence Agency in Cambodia as the war in neighbouring South Vietnam began to have a bearing on regional security. In 1965, Australia's foreign minister, Paul Hasluck, authorised the establishment of an ASIS station in the Cambodian capital, Phnom Penh, in anticipation of a decision by the country's ruler, Prince Norodom Sihanouk, to sever ties with the United States. When diplomatic relations were eventually severed and the American Embassy was closed, an undeclared ASIS officer and operational assistant took over the network of agents formerly being run by the Central Intelligence Agency (CIA). According to an unauthorised history of ASIS, the CIA conceded that ASIS engaged in 'unique operations and reporting' in Cambodia. The Australian effort was considered 'one of the four most important contributions the Service [ASIS] had made over the years to the agency's requirements.[13]

In response to this declassification request, the ASIS argued that to confirm or deny the existence of those records (dating back to 1969), would cause damage to Australia's national interests – 50 years later. ASIS sought a Public Interest Certificate in order to make its case in secret, resisting attempts by the applicant to test the strength and cogency of the claim under cross-examination. ASIS stated that confirming the existence of any ASIS records would have the effect of disclosing that the agency had an interest in the subject. Apparently, it would be contrary to the public interest to disclose that ASIS had an interest in any country unless the Australian Government officially confirmed such interest. Such an understanding of what constitutes the public interest echoes the mindset of an earlier era when the very existence of ASIS was kept secret. It was not until October 1977 that the Prime Minister, Malcolm Fraser, delivered a Ministerial Statement acknowledging its existence. The agency asserted that it would be contrary to the public interest to declassify records or simply to 'sanitise' them by redacting the identity of sources while retaining the essence of the content. The records remain beyond the reach of researchers.

In sum, the Public Interest Certificates issued by various Attorneys-General have prevented the testing in open courts of potentially exaggerated claims that release of public records might damage Australia's security, defence or international relations. To stress the point again: Public Interest Certificates are self-executing within proceedings of the Administrative Appeals Tribunal. Once the Attorney-General issues a Certificate, the Tribunal is required to exclude everyone other than the relevant intelligence agency or government department, from the room while the matter is considered. No competing or contrary view is heard by the AAT members.

The nature of the AAT

The AAT has authority under legislation to review the administrative decisions made by Australian Government ministers, departments and agencies. Applicants and respondents who appear before the AAT are responsible for their own legal costs. A contrast is the Federal Court of Australia where costs may be awarded against the losing side. In that sense, resorting to proceedings before the AAT are less of a deterrent than seeking judicial review of a decision by the National Archives to refuse access to an official record.

Notably, the AAT is not a court within the meaning of Chapter III of the Commonwealth Constitution. Federal Labor and Coalition governments have consistently appointed a large number of former politicians and ministerial staffers to the AAT, qualified for appointment only by their party political backgrounds. Former High Court judge, Ian Callinan, reviewed the Abbott Government's decision in 2015 to amalgamate the AAT with the Migration Review Tribunal, the Refugee Review Tribunal and the Social Security Appeal Tribunal. His report to Parliament was tabled in July 2019. It was scathing in its criticism of what could only be termed political appointments. Callinan recommended that 'all further appointments, re-appointments or renewals of appointment to the membership of the AAT should be of lawyers, admitted or qualified for admission to a Supreme Court of a State or Territory or the High Court of Australia, and on the basis of merit'. With many political appointees out of their depth in terms of the law and legal processes, Callinan noted that AAT staff often dictated decisions to inexperienced and inexpert Tribunal members. Callinan criticised this practice: 'There is no need for, and it is not appropriate that Registry staff, whether by preparing "templates" for decisions, or giving "legal advice" to Members, participate in making or writing, or assisting in writing, decisions by Members'.[14]

Despite the proposed reforms, the fact remains that the AAT is not a Chapter III court. Its members do not enjoy the same security of tenure as judges and their capacity to make informed and independent decisions is potentially impaired by the nature of their appointment and the jurisdiction they exercise.

A proposal for a Public Interest Advocates system

How might competing claims about where the public interest might lie in security matters be resolved? A possible solution to the problem of information alleged to be too sensitive for disclosure on national security grounds is the appointment of a 'Public Interest Advocate' with both 'disclosure' and 'representative' functions. Consistent with this general line of thinking, a Public Interest Advocate would assist the AAT in declassification cases involving national security information when exemption was sought by the governnent.

The Public Interest Advocate (PIA) would *not* be a lawyer for the applicant. I am not suggesting the government provide a pro bono representative for those wanting access to documents. Rather, the PIA's role would be considering the applicant's interests *and* those of the Australian public. It is a mistake to think the government's lawyers represent the public when their remit is to act on the state's behalf. The state briefs them and pays them. My point is that the public and the state may not have converging interests. The state can also act in a self-interested way over and possibly against those from whom its authority to govern is derived.

The 'disclosure' function would enable the PIA to challenge any objection from the National Archives that disclosing material would prejudice security. The 'representative' function would allow the PIA to examine and challenge confidential material which cannot be disclosed to the applicant. I accept that a possible weakness in my proposal is a continuing prohibition on the PIA disclosing any confidential material to the applicant or receiving instructions from an applicant about how to interpret or assess such material, thus limiting the applicant's ability to test any adverse evidence. But they should be able to take an adversarial approach to whatever the government might tender as evidence for non-disclosure.

To discharge their responsibilities, PIAs would need access to independent expertise and supporting evidence. They would require adequate resources, both intellectual and financial. They must be able to call witnesses. They must have resort to acceptable rules of evidence that exclude unattributed assertions and unidentifiable claims made by intelligence agencies. Such rules would need to be sufficiently robust to require timely disclosure by the agencies. PIAs would be assisted by a secretariat and access to a searchable database of the AAT's closed judgments. The latter provision would allow PIAs to build and retain corporate memory within an experienced PIA community.

Arriving at the public interest – concluding observations

I have gained the clear impression that speculation over what constitutes damage to national security is often contingent on the speculator's personal perspective and preferred outcomes. An intelligence official who is instinctively hostile to declassification can readily construct a framework of belief that makes this hostility eminently reasonable. Academics and media commentators whose instincts lean towards order rather than justice often do the same thing. For them, political stability ought to be a first order concern. They can – and usually do – work within a system of belief that justifies such an attitude without difficulty. Furthermore, they are usually persuaded by the complete integrity of their position. The same is likely true of those who elevate the demands of justice over order, and then call for the declassification of official records.

These are not new ideas. As Bertrand Russell once remarked:

> Reason has a perfectly clear and precise meaning. It signifies the choice of the right means to an end that you wish to achieve. It has nothing whatever to do with the choice of ends. … Desires, emotions, passions (you can choose whichever word you will), are the only possible causes of action. Reason is not a cause of action but only a regulator.[15]

Russell's observations stand in the tradition of David Hume's contention that 'reason is, and ought only to be the slave of the passions, and can never pretend to any other office than to serve and obey them.'[16] There is no Archimedean point from which we can make value-free judgments. Indeed, most judgments rely on values whether or not we are conscious of their operation.

How, then, might the impasse I have described be adequately resolved? The appointment of Public Interest Advocates would certainly be a valuable corrective to the lop-sidedness of the current system. The existence of PIAs would stand against the possibility of Attorneys-General being dazzled by overblown claims about sensitivity, risk and security. Just because a document touches on intelligence gathering, there is no need for law officers to reach reflexively for a Public Interest Certificate without a second thought as to whether the matter would harm the Commonwealth. I suspect, however, that the proposal for a Public Interest Advocate system will be received in the same way as the original application for declassification – those who are instinctively pro-declassification will find ways to agree with the proposal. Those on the other side will likely do the opposite – with a well-constructed belief system to justify the desired outcome. Acknowledging that beliefs and values are integral to our handling of this matter would be a small step towards a realistic discussion of what is really at stake and why.

Endnotes

1　S. 33 (1) (a) and s 33 (1) (b) of the *Archives Act* 1983.

2　*Fernandes v National Archives of Australia* [2011] AATA 202; *Fernandes v National Archives of Australia* [2014] AATA 180; *National Archives of Australia v Fernandes* [2014] FCAFC 158.

3　S. 40 (8), *Archives Act* 1983.

4　Jeffrey T Richelson and Desmond Ball, *The Ties That Bind: Intelligence Cooperation Between the UKUSA Countries - the United Kingdom, the United States of America, Canada, Australia and New Zealand*, Allen & Unwin, Sydney, 1985; Brian Toohey and Marian Wilkinson, *The Book of Leaks: Exposes in Defence of the Public's Right to Know*, Angus and Robertson, Sydney, 1987; Department of the Parliamentary Library, *Balibo revisited - the deaths of five journalists in East Timor*, Parliamentary Library Information Service, Canberra, 1995; Tom Sherman, *Report on the deaths of Australian-based journalists in East Timor in 1975*, Department of Foreign Affairs and Trade, Canberra, 1996; Tom Sherman, *Second report on the deaths of Australian-based journalists in East Timor in 1975*, Department of Foreign Affairs and Trade, Canberra, 1999; Desmond Ball & Hamish McDonald, *Death in Balibo, Lies in Canberra*, Allen & Unwin, St Leonards, 2000; Wendy Way (ed.), *Documents on Australian Foreign Policy: Australia and the Indonesian Incorporation of Portuguese Timor, 1974–1976*, Department of Foreign Affairs and Trade/Melbourne University Press, Carlton, 2000; NSW Coroner, *Inquest into the death of Brian Raymond Peters*, New South Wales Coroner's Court, Sydney, 2007.

5　Richard Woolcott, *Minute to Alan Renouf*, 24 September 1974. National Archives of Australia, Commonwealth Record Series A11443, Portuguese Timor: July-September 1974.

6　Walter Miller, *Minute to Alan Renouf*, 17 September 1975. NAA: A1838, 3038/10/1, xxxi. Portuguese Timor: relations with and policy towards.

7　For more discussion, see Miranda Booth, *Pritchett's Prediction: Australian foreign policy toward Indonesia's incorporation of East Timor, 1974–1999*, MPhil thesis, UNSW Canberra, 2017.

8　Clinton Fernandes, *The Independence of East Timor: Multidimensional Perspectives*, Sussex Academic Press, Eastbourne, 2011, p. 41.

9　Sarah Staveteig, 'How Many Persons in East Timor Went 'Missing' During the Indonesian Occupation? Results from Indirect Estimates', International Institute for Applied Systems Analysis, Austria, 2007.

10　S. 36, *Administrative Appeals Tribunal Act* 1975.

11　Letter from the Attorney-General of Australia to Clinton Fernandes, 9 September 2010. Copy in the author's possession.

12　For example, see Robert J Hanyok, *Spartans in Darkness: American SIGINT and the Indochina War, 1945–1975*, Center for Cryptologic History, National Security Agency, 2002.

13　Brian Toohey and William Pinwill, *Oyster: The Story of the Australian Secret Intelligence Service*, William Heinemann, Port Melbourne, 1989, pp. 126–133. See also Phillip

Knightley, 'Grit in the Oyster', *Best of The Independent Monthly*, Deakin University Press, Geelong, 1992, pp. 155–59.

14   Ian Callinan, Review: section 4 of the Tribunals Amalgamation Act 2015 (Cth), 2019. Available at https://www.ag.gov.au/Consultations/Documents/statutory-review-tribunals-act-2015/report-statutory-review-aat.pdf.

15   Bertrand Russell, *Human Society in Ethics and Politics*, Allen and Unwin, London, 1954, p. 8.

16   David Hume, *A Treatise of Human Nature: Being an Attempt to introduce the experimental Method of Reasoning into Moral Subjects*, Penguin, Hammondsworth, 1969.

CHAPTER 9

Effectiveness, efficiency and the public interest: the case of the ADF

Chip Saint

L eadership studies can never be static. General Stanley McChrystal, the former commander of United States Joint Special Operations Command, recently observed:

> Leadership needs to be redefined for the modern age to consider how humans actually behave. It needs to take into account the relationship between leaders and followers in a particular situation and in a specific context. Because the situation and context matter so much, checklists and formulas are not all that helpful to us when we try to study leadership, emulate leadership or train others to lead.[1]

Changes in technology and work force character have always challenged leaders. The successful preparation of leaders to meet these challenges requires constant attention to how and why workplace situations and contexts change. Implementing changes to leadership preparation is a vital component to ensuring an organisation remains fit for purpose. All work places are different and what is effective in one work place may not be in another. The military work place is like no other.

Few Australians work in an environment where death is considered an acceptable hazard in the course of fulfilling a mission statement. Similarly, few are in a workplace where you are trained, equipped and expected to kill your competitors, destroy their infrastructure and to do so with lethal intent and overwhelming force. How many people do you know whose failure to achieve their mission statement might imperil the integrity of the nation? There is no-one to pick up the slack if you fail; you are the last line of defence. The mission statement of the Australian Army is to prepare land forces for war in order to defend Australia and its national interests. The Army, as with every element of the Australian Defence Force (ADF), is tasked with pursuing the nation's interest by maintaining a credible military capability and without such a capability the common good is threatened.

To produce a workforce that is ready, willing and able of meeting the 'unlimited liability' of the public good, the nation expects volunteers from among the citizenry to undergo specific training and the enculturation of certain values and not only to pass physical tests but also to achieve standards in the engrained exercise of courage, initiative, respect and team work.[2] Those who answer the nation's call to a military vocation also expect to relinquish a portion of their personal freedom and to have their every action reconciled with the common law and the *Defence Force Discipline Act* 1982 (DFDA). In short, uniformed personnel must anticipate being the target of lethal force and possibly being killed, ordering others to shoot and kill, being liable to be fined or imprisoned for transgressing laws requiring standards of conduct that only apply to military members, undergo tests of physical, moral and ethical courage, and to do so without compulsion.

In this context, producing this force and leading those who apply it has its challenges. Fortunately, the ADF has had time to develop and refine the training and education required to transform a citizen into a combatant. From Federation in 1901 to the wars in Iraq and Afghanistan, this training and education has been adapted to meet changes in situation and in context. By most objective measures, the ADF has successfully produced soldiers and officers who have protected the nation and promoted its interests. The training involves many things but, primarily, it enculturates the individual into an ethos of service which foregrounds sacrifice.

The cultural alignment of the workforce is the vital component in the ADF's effectiveness. When this alignment is underpinned by the DFDA's coercive power, the Army's hierarchical model of leader-follower allows it to undertake a warfighting role effectively and efficiently. The ADF is at its optimum capability when it is 'uniformly uniformed', by which I mean when its workforce consists entirely of uniformed personnel.

The contemporary Defence workforce is not, however, 'uniformly uniformed'. Instead, Defence has become a combined uniformed-civilian workforce and for good public interest reasons. With this change in situation and in context, it is important to examine whether the leadership model, developed in an era when the relationship between the leader and the led was less complex in a more hierarchical society, is still fit for purpose. My interest lies in the consequences of these public interest decisions on the composition of the military workforce and how military leaders lead that workforce. Before delving into the leadership issues, however, it is important to understand how and why the military workforce has changed.

★ ★ ★ ★

The genesis of the transition to a mixed workforce can be traced to a series of studies commencing 30 years ago. In late 1989, Alan Wrigley, a former RAAF officer, public servant and Director-General of ASIO, was asked by the then Defence Minister, Kim Beazley, to undertake a review of civil-military relationships.[3] Wrigley's Terms of Reference directed him to 'explore how the Australian community could play a greater role in strengthening Australia's security and how more weight could be given to the Government's policy of eliminating unnecessary duplication of civil and military skills and capabilities.'[4]

In commissioning Wrigley, Beazley was attempting to address a fundamental question in public spending: does the pursuit of efficiency or the maintenance of effectiveness have primacy? For most elements of government spending, adopting the pursuit of efficiency maintains primacy because it incurs little or no risk. Resources can be seen to be saved and, when deficiencies are identified, they can be rectified. Some elements of government spending, such as Defence, do not however lend themselves easily to such a decision. The ramifications of taking the incorrect approach can be dire if the right balance is not struck. Too big a focus on efficiency can lead to hubris and unpreparedness for contingencies. Maintaining effectiveness, on the other hand, is very costly and particularly difficult for politicians to justify in peacetime.

Wrigley may not have been the first to consider the question of whether to pursue efficiency or maintain effectiveness in ensuring the security of the nation but he was among the most influential. Minister Beazley's motivation for initiating Wrigley's review was twofold. The first was to 'seek ways of having the Australian community' take part in the defence of the nation.[5] The second was to 'identify opportunities for greater efficiency ... in countering military threats to Australia's security, through use of capabilities and capacities that exist or might yet be developed in the Australian community'.[6] Wrigley was given scope to analyse the extent to which civil infrastructure[7] was currently being used in the nation's defence planning and to how more extensive use by Defence of the civil infrastructure could enhance the nation's ability to meet a series of contingencies.[8] In this case, civil infrastructure was considered to be human capacity and capability, as well as types and locations of businesses, transport structures and routes, and communications companies and architecture.[9] The resulting report, *Defence and the Community: A Partnership in Australia's Defence*, better known by its eponymous title, the 'Wrigley Report', was tabled in June 1990 and formed the basis for the 1991 Commercial Support Program (CSP). The CSP ultimately oversaw the transfer of upwards of 10,000 military and Defence civilian positions to the private sector.[10]

Wrigley was shaped by almost two decades of post-Vietnam War thinking on Defence matters. By way of background, in the 1970s, two new but fundamental concepts of the ADF were developed. First, in 1972, the McMahon Government's *Australian Defence Review* recognised the requirement for an element of 'self-reliance' in the nation's defence.[11] Self-reliance was balanced by efforts to develop and maintain strategic alliances, most importantly with the United States. Second, the successor Whitlam Government ended obligatory military service making the ADF an all-volunteer Force.[12] The 1976 Defence White Paper (DWP76) formalised these concepts and declared 'that Australia no longer based its defence policy on the expectations that its Navy, Army and Air Force would be "sent abroad to fight as part of some other nation's forces".[13] In his analysis of DWP76, Alan Stephens argued that, within five years, its ability to set the Defence planning agenda had largely ended. Stephens identified the inability of the government to 'define its strategic objectives and to set realistic financial projections' as the reasons for its demise as a planning tool.[14]

By the time of Wrigley's review in 1989, aimlessness seems to have pervaded Defence strategic planning. Public support for Defence remained high, but public interest in the policy debate had steadily waned. To re-energise public debate, the Hawke Government initiated two important reviews in 1986; one into defence capability and the other into industry's ability to support defence.[15] The Dibb Review of Australia's defence capability found that 'the key difficulty ... is that the [Defence] Department and the ADF do not agree on the appropriate level of conflict against which we should structure the Defence Force'.[16] The Cooksey Review into industry's capacity to support defence revealed a 'distinct lack of policy coordination in relation to overall strategic defence policy, which determines both force structure and policy for defence industry'.[17] The task of trying to correct elements of this misalignment was addressed in DWP87.

DWP87 asserted that Australia faced 'no presently identifiable military threat, except for the remote possibility of global war'.[18] Priority was given to denying an adversary the air and sea approaches to Australia. Defence acquisition was focussed on building the intelligence architecture and on air and maritime platforms. This acquisition was deemed to be the most prudent given the prevailing lack of strategic clarity. In 1986, Dibb had called for an average Defence budget of 3 percent of GDP.[19] DWP87 recommended a modest 2.6 per cent of GDP and Defence actually received 2.5 percent in FY 87–88 which fell to 2 percent the following year. Not for the first, nor last, time, Defence acquisition outran the money available. To rectify the shortfall, Beazley announced that Defence would need to fund part of its acquisition costs through internal departmental savings. In the absence of an identifiable threat to the nation that would have driven defence spending higher, Defence instead began the search for efficiencies.

The DWP87 also re-affirmed the policy of self-reliance. In his introduction to DWP87, Defence Minister Beazley stated that 'self-reliance is a task involving the whole nation ... Australian industry will be called upon to involve itself more intensively in the support, maintenance and development of Australia's Defence Force'.[20] With military and Australian Public Service personnel costs accounting for in excess of 35 percent of the total Defence budget, it is not surprising that the two guiding imperatives, finding efficiencies and a policy of self-reliance, led Wrigley's review in 1989 inexorably towards the concept of commercialisation.

Wrigley highlighted one other consideration that would ultimately settle the argument of efficiency versus effectiveness. Wrigley emphasised that successive reviews had all found that 'outside of a direct superpower clash more significant military challenges could emerge only after years of growing tension and diplomatic failure'.[21] In contrast, the prevailing view within the ADF was the need to prepare for a 'come as you are' war, the argument for maintaining effectiveness. Wrigley felt the ADF's mindset completely disregarded the notion that antecedent actions, measured in years and well within the capability of our intelligence architecture to provide strategic warning, would provide sufficient time to build a more capable military force, a view consistent with the pursuit of the efficiency argument.

While all of the strategic documents pointed to the efficiency argument and served to justify Wrigley's promotion of commercialisation, he did warn that 'these matters can have important effects on the way the force-in-being is trained, structured and supported: they call for different solutions from those which would simply maximise the utility of that force'.[22] Wrigley elaborated further saying,

> the review has assumed future Australian governments would not require the defence force to conduct large scale independent military operations beyond the effective reach of Australia's supporting national infrastructure. Without these assumptions, the scope for involving the Australian community and its public and commercial infrastructure more in providing for the security of the nation would be considerably limited.[23]

Wrigley understood that, by pursuing efficiency, he was potentially limiting the effectiveness of the ADF. It was a conscious trade-off.

Three decades later, there have been a series of reviews and reports that have all approached the issue of reducing inefficiency and service duplication with commercial outsourcing. The goal of this outsourcing was to 'achieve private sector productivity levels through competition and high-power incentives for cost-minimisation'.[24] While this trend has met the public interest test of cost effectiveness in Defence spending, one of the practical consequences is more and more contractors are joining the previously 'uniformly uniformed' workforce.

It is difficult to ascertain the actual number of contractors currently employed by the Department of Defence. The difficulty is two-fold. First, the term, 'contractor', is not readily defined by the Department of Defence. It is variously used to describe consultants, civilian service providers and labour hire companies.[25] The second is the absence of a separate line item for contractors in the Defence Budget Statement expressed as a total number of people and a total dollar cost, as it is with the cost of ADF and APS members. The total contractor cost is a component of 'Sustainment' and only appears as a dollar figure.[26] The closest approximation of the total number of contractors was provided in 2017 when the then Secretary of the Department of Defence, Dennis Richardson, informed his staff that upwards of 18,000 'contractors, consultants and service providers' were employed by the Department.[27] At the same time, the number of APS members in the Department of Defence was 17,728.[28] Indeed, if Richardson's number was accurate, contractors made up the second largest group within Defence after the Army.[29] Is this a problem? Possibly.

Any policy or decision involving taxpayer money must be conscious of delivering value for money but that principle cannot be allowed to disqualify or disable the objective. What is the point of having an ADF if it cannot fight? It could be inexpensive but it could leave the nation without viable defences against real adversaries. My research could not uncover an approach or a metric for determining whether efficiency has come at the expense of effectiveness in relation to defence preparedness and operational success. It is possible to measure the cost of an activity in human and material terms but nations continue to struggle with assessments before, during and after an operation on the question of whether a desire to maximise taxpayer resources was at the expense of another public interest: winning the fight. It is another case of measuring what can be measured and not measuring what matters. Why invest at all if the minimal investment is more token than intention?

There are practical reasons why governments focus on efficiency. Efficiency is measurable. It is here and now. It is also an expression of political will. As we have seen, Wrigley pursued efficiency and ultimately saved the Department of Defence, and the taxpayers of Australia, millions of dollars in expenditure. His, and subsequent reviews, moved ADF personnel out of support roles and into fighting roles, maximising the efficiency of the manpower-capped, volunteer force. An inquiry in 1998 by the Joint Parliamentary Committee on Foreign Affairs, Defence and Trade supported Wrigley's approach by noting:

> The logic for personnel reduction initiatives is clear. Many non-core support functions can be supplied more cheaply through commercialisa-tion, and reliance on civilian outsourcing makes sound financial sense in a peacetime environment. Currently planned reductions within the ADF are directed toward support areas such as catering, stores and maintenance, allowing redirection of resources to expand the number of personnel in more combat-related roles.[30]

Wrigley did recognise, however, this would affect to some degree the effective-ness of the ADF. But just how would effectiveness be measured? Ultimately, the effectiveness of the ADF is measured against its ability to meet any enduring obligation to fight and win the nation's wars. This is a high-risk metric as any failure has dire consequences for national sovereignty. Fortunately for Australia, the ADF has not been tested to this extent since the Wrigley Review. Perhaps the only test came during the ADF-led intervention in East Timor (the Democratic Republic of Timor Leste since May 2002) in 1999.[31]

The ADF-led intervention into East Timor provided an opportunity to judge the effectiveness of the ADF in responding to contingency. Few could argue that the commander of the International Force East Timor (INTERFET), the then Major-General Peter Cosgrove, and his INTERFET force, achieved a remarkably effective outcome in providing a stable security environment for the people of East Timor while delicately balancing the relationship with the Indonesian military. There is ample evidence to conclude that at the individual level, the sailors, soldiers and airmen and women of the ADF performed superbly. This vindicated the effectiveness of concentrating uni-formed ADF members towards the more operational end of the ADF. The impact of concentrating uniformed ADF members towards the operational components did have a debilitating impact, however, on the ability of the ADF to support itself effectively.

A study of logistical support to the intervention force during the East Timor crisis that was conducted by the Australian National Audit Office (ANAO) thought the task was 'as easy as it gets'.[32] This view was based on the close geographic proximity of the East Timor theatre of operations to the Australian mainland, the relatively small size of the theatre of operations, the absence of sustained combat and no enemy interference with the logistics supply chain, and no large scale manoeuvre of combat forces. Despite all of these favourable factors, the ANAO found:

> The East Timor deployments occurred after more than a decade of Defence peacetime reform and rationalisation that had brought about significant reductions in personnel (including logistics personnel) in Defence. The deployments highlighted severe limitations in the ADF in critical skill areas. Systemic logistic and strategic movement weaknesses had been identified in previous ADF deployments offshore, such as Somalia and Papua New Guinea, but had not been remedied. When the East Timor crisis developed, Defence's logistic structures, systems and processes did not prove suitable to support the military deployments.[33]

Major-General Cosgrove's submission to the ANAO review provided a characteristically blunt battlefield commander's view:

> In the past the Australian armed forces have not had to invest in substantial deployable logistic capabilities. Our forces have relied on our major allies such as the United States and Britain. The logistic support for INTERFET was magnificent, but sustainment was not achieved without frustration and some failures. Frankly, if the ADF is required by the nation to go offshore again in a lead role or as a contributor to international military action, we will have to underwrite our operations with a responsive and effective logistic system with stamina. At the moment there is room for enhancement of our capability to support offshore operations. We succeeded in East Timor but our logistic engine was under extreme pressure most of the time.[34]

At the commencement of the East Timor intervention in 1999, the logistics capability in the Army was in a parlous state.[35] In the 10 years following

Wrigley and the CSP, the logistics capability had atrophied as resources were drawn away from the ADF logistics capability and towards the operational end of the ADF. The chart below is drawn from the ANAO report and indicates the decline in personnel numbers in the Army's primary logistics corps during the past decade.[36]

Personnel numbers in Army's primary logistics corps

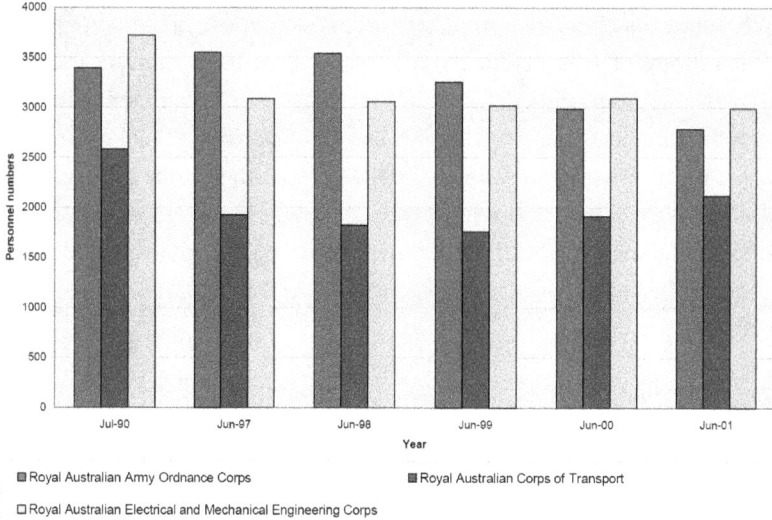

▨ Royal Australian Army Ordnance Corps	▧ Royal Australian Corps of Transport
▢ Royal Australian Electrical and Mechanical Engineering Corps	

While some of the personnel losses were attributed to advances in technology, commercialisation had taken over many of the logistics roles. The ANAO's examination of contractors highlighted:

> there are two significant obstacles to the use of civil contractors in areas of military operations. These concern delays and costs in preparing civilians to meet Defence requirements for deployment, and the potential liability involved in having civilians working for Defence in a non-secure environment. Legal obligations and Defence security arrangements under which commercial suppliers have to work in areas of operation had not previously been documented. Lack of guidance for engagement of civilians in support of the ADF in East Timor and concern for their safety caused Defence to minimise the involvement of civilian contractors in East Timor. However, Defence made timely and

> effective use of contractors in establishing valuable telecommunication
> links in East Timor early in the deployments.[37]

Anecdotal evidence from ADF veterans of East Timor has generally confirmed a similar story. Most veterans identified that support mechanisms to individual units, in particular catering and logistics, was limited and became a cause for concern.[38] This view was supported in *A Military History of Australia*, which found the logistics system 'was stretched almost to breaking point' and there were significant shortcomings in 'long-range communications ... and engineering capabilities'.[39] The pursuit of efficiency in commercialisation of support functions appeared to have had an effect on the ADF's ability to support itself. What cannot be overlooked is that the Timor intervention provided only a simple and relatively short test of the ADF's effectiveness. A longer campaign further from the Australian supply chain would have placed crippling pressure on the capacity of the ADF to undertake its mission effectively.

Effectiveness can also be viewed over time. Tracing the development of the ADF through the various reviews and DWPs after Vietnam, Jeffery Grey highlights a litany of mistakes and adverse impacts on ADF capability. Most dramatically, he notes the May 1998 fire aboard HMAS *Westralia*, caused by a failure of a fuel-line in the engine room, in which four naval personnel were killed. He concludes, 'the accident was related to the privatisation of support services and a corresponding decline in maintenance standards'.[40] This isolated incident perhaps went to the heart of the effectiveness vs efficiency debate. In an organisation such as Defence, how is a balance achieved between the inescapable requirement for efficiency with the absolute requirement to maintain effectiveness? While Wrigley and the plethora of subsequent reviews and inquiries can provide reasoned arguments for one over the other, the ultimate decision rests with elected officials. Defence could work towards improving internal efficiencies without ministerial direction. It seldom, if ever occurs. It is my observation that everything about the ADF is geared towards achieving maximum efficiency. The task of the ADF is to interpret these shifts and then adapt as the situation and the context changes.

✷ ✷ ✷ ✷

Within ADF units both deploying and stationed at home, an increasing number of contractors have started to challenge workforce relationships and the culture that ultimately delivers lethal force in pursuit of national objectives. Instead of a traditionally mono-culturally aligned workforce, the military workplace must now grapple with two inconsistent or contested cultures – one committed to the national interest and the other to shareholder interests. As a leader of this workforce, rather than relying on traditional hierarchical leadership and the coercive power of the DFDA to motivate and lead a mixed community of people, I have derived some useful insights from what is known as the 'principal – agent problem' in determining how and when to use extrinsic motivators, such as financial incentives and rewards, and deciding when to wield the contractual obligation stick.

The workforce I lead is very different to the one I was trained to lead more than a quarter of a century ago. My workplace, the Army Aviation Training Centre (AAvnTC) at Oakey in Southeast Queensland, is responsible for training rotary wing pilots, aircrew and maintenance personnel for the Australian Army and the Royal Australian Navy. The AAvnTC has approximately 300 instructional and administrative staff. The leadership group at the AAvnTC are Australian Army officers and Warrant Officers. In keeping with the traditional ADF leadership model, there is a single commander, accountable to the Chief of Army for the safe and efficient running of the AAvnTC. That commander is the Commandant of the Army Aviation Training Centre (COMDT AAvnTC), an Army Aviation Colonel, an experienced pilot and commissioned officer with at least 25 years of military experience. As in all military organisations, the COMDT discharges expectations levied by superiors and subordinates. These expectations are imposed on the COMDT as an individual. Discharging them is his sole responsibility as the accountable commander. The COMDT has the military training and experience to understand, interpret, accept and effectively meet these expectations. These expectations only cover the ADF workforce, however. At the AAvnTC, contractors comprise half the instructional staff, a large component of the sustainment staff, and almost all of the emergency response staff.

By contrast, the expectations of the contractor component require the COMDT to accept additional responsibilities and accept external authorities. These additional responsibilities and external authorities are complicated and emerging issues for military commanders. Unlike the traditional disciplined hierarchical expectations of superior and subordinate, contractor expectations are actually expectations of partnership. To understand this complexity fully, the scope of the partnership needs to be recognised and ultimately reconciled. First, contractors are a service provider to the COMDT delivering direct training of pilots and aircrew, and providing aircraft maintenance. Second, contractors are customers of the COMDT in that they rely on the Defence supply chain, engineering and authorisations to perform their roles. Third, contractors are tenants of the COMDT on the Oakey Defence base with interests in base plans, security and workplace behaviours.

Finally, contractors belong to prime contracting companies with business dealings beyond Oakey. The broader reputation of the companies can be affected by comments or actions of the COMDT or those ADF officers speaking or acting on his behalf. These partnership expectations are difficult to address because they represent a departure from the normal military leadership model which rests on a single accountable individual. Partnerships imply shared responsibilities and diverging accountabilities. With partnerships between the military and contractors becoming more common, this will test the traditional military leadership model.

Noting the rapidly and profoundly changing workplace, a re-think is needed of how military leaders are trained so that financial efficiency and operational effectiveness can be held in creative tension. They are ultimately compatible if the focus is on service delivery *and* mission success. The Army cannot compromise its ability to meet the public interest requirement of fighting and winning this nation's wars. At the same time, maximising the cost efficiency of the Army through outsourcing is plainly in the public interest as well.

As the workforce dynamic has changed to foreground the pursuit of these two public interest goals in tandem, increasing pressure is being placed on military leaders to ensure they are sufficiently flexible to inspire and lead this more variegated workforce. This flexibility will require a broader approach to the teaching and subsequent recognising of military officers who succeed in leading this blended workforce. The Defence workplace has fundamentally changed in situation and context. As General McChrystal, whose observations I quoted at the opening of this chapter, highlights, when our situation and context change, there is a pressing need to review our traditional leadership models to ensure they remain fit for purpose. My doctoral research is aimed at providing the ADF with leadership training models that are.

Endnotes

1   Stanley McChrystal, 'Everything I thought About Leadership Has Changed', *From the Green Notebook*, 01 November, 2018, https://fromthegreennotebook.com/2018/11/01/mcchrystal-everything-i-thought-about-leadership-has-changed/ accessed 01 July 2019.
2   These are the formally promulgated Australian Army Values.
3   Alan K Wrigley, *The Defence Force and the Community: A partnership in Australia's Defence,* Australian Government Publishing Services, Canberra, 1990, Appendix A.
4   Wrigley, *The Defence Force and the Community*, Appendix A.
5   Wrigley, *The Defence Force and the Community*, Appendix A.
6   Wrigley, *The Defence Force and the Community*, Appendix A.
7   Wrigley's review was initially titled, 'The use of civil infrastructure in Australia's Defence', Wrigley, *The Defence Force and the Community*, Appendix A.
8   Wrigley, *The Defence Force and the Community*, Appendix A.
9   Wrigley, *The Defence Force and the Community*, Appendix A.
10 Henry Ergas and Mark Thomson, 'More guns without less butter: improving Australian defence efficiency', *Agenda: A Journal of Policy Analysis and Reform*, ANU, 2011, p. 36.
11 David Fairbairn, *Australian defence: Ministerial Statement,* 1972, https://parlinfo.aph.gov.au/parlInfo/search/display/display.w3p;query=Id%3A%22hansard80%2Fhansardr80%2F1972-04–20%2F0053%22;src1=sm1, accessed 16 Jun 19.
12 Nicole Brangwin et al, *Defending Australia: a history of Australia's Defence White Papers,* Parliamentary Library Research Paper, 20 Aug 2015, p. 10.
13 Brangwin et al, *Defending Australia*, p. 12.
14 Brangwin et al, *Defending Australia*, p. 15.
15 Brangwin et al, *Defending Australia*, p. 17.
16 Paul Dibb, *Review of Australia's Defence Capabilities*, Australian Government Publishing Service, Canberra, March 1986, p. vi, accessed 11 June 2019.
17 RJ Cooksey, *Review of Australia's defence exports and defence industry,* Australian Government Publishing Service, Canberra, 17 October 1986, p. 53.
18 Australian Government, *1987 Defence White Paper: The Defence of Australia*, Australian Government Publishing Service, p. 30.

19   Dibb, *Review of Australia's Defence Capabilities*, pp. 172–73.

20   *1987 Defence White Paper: The Defence of Australia*, pp ix, x.

21   Wrigley, *The Defence Force and the Community*, p.46.

22   Wrigley, *The Defence Force and the Community*, p. 49.

23   Wrigley, *The Defence Force and the Community*, p 60.

24   Ergas and Thomson, 'More guns without less butter', p. 34.

25   Rather than try to define what a contractor is, it is more useful to describe what a contractor is not. I consider a contractor to mean any human employed by the Department of Defence who is not in uniform or employed under the *Public Service Act*.

26   Sustainment is the 'provision of the appropriate goods and services required to achieve readiness and sustainability goals for the life of the Defence Element. Defence Sustainment involves the provision of in service support, including repair and maintenance, engineering, supply and replacement parts, configuration management and disposal action. Sustainment can apply to platforms (ships, aircraft, vehicle fleets), commodities (clothing, combat rations, munitions) or services (calibration, provision of maritime target ranges)'. Department of Defence submission to the Joint Committee of Public Accounts and Audit Inquiry into Defence sustainment expenditure, February 2017, p. 2.

27   Sally Whyte, 'Contractors ranks soar at Defence', *Canberra Times*, 12 December 2018, p. 3.

28   Australian Government, *Budget Review 2019–2020*, Workforce, Table 3, Total Workforce https://www.aph.gov.au/About_Parliament/Parliamentary_Departments/Parliamentary_Library/pubs/rp/BudgetReview201920/Defence, accessed 30 Jun 2019.

29   According to the Defence Portfolio budget statement for 2019 – 2020, there were 14,776 Navy personnel 30,821 Army personnel and 14,493 Air Force personnel. http://www.defence.gov.au/Budget/19–20/2019-20_Defence_PBS_00_Complete.pdf, accessed 30 June 2019.

30   Joint Parliamentary Committee on Foreign Affairs Defence and Trade Report, *Funding Australia's Defence*, 8 May 1998, https://www.aph.gov.au/Parliamentary_Business/Committees/House_of_Representatives_Committees?url=jfadt/def_funding/reportind.htm .

31   I have deliberately avoided mentioning the more recent campaigns in Afghanistan and Iraq. These deployments were undertaken in coalition with the United States and ADF elements were able to utilise the much bigger American supply system. East Timor offered the closest example of defence 'self-reliance', an underpinning principle of Wrigley's review.

32   Australian National Audit Office (ANAO), *Management of Australian Defence Force Deployments to East Timor*, Audit Report no. 38, Department of Defence, Canberra, 2002, p. 52.

33   ANAO, *Management of Australian Defence Force Deployments to East Timor*, pp. 86–87.

34   ANAO, *Management of Australian Defence Force Deployments to East Timor*, p. 62.

35   David Beaumont, 'Logistics and the Failure to Modernise', *On Ops: Lessons and Challenges for the Australian Army since East Timor*, Tom Frame and Albert Palazzo (eds), UNSW Press, 2016, p.138.

36   ANAO, *Management of Australian Defence Force Deployments to East Timor*, pp. 53–54.

37   ANAO, *Management of Australian Defence Force Deployments to East Timor*, p. 85.

38   I also hold this view. I served with the 6th Battalion Group in East Timor in 2000. The ability to provide fresh food to a battalion on operations was limited by a lack of uniformed cooks and a very narrow supply chain. .

39   Jeffery Grey, *A Military History of Australia*, third edition, Cambridge University Press, 2008, p. 278.

40   Grey, *A Military History of Australia*, p. 274.

CHAPTER 10

Police officers or law enforcers?

Clement O'Regan

As a police officer serving at the Headquarters of the Queensland Police in Brisbane, when I drove to work each morning it would be normal for me to see dozens of breaches of the traffic law along that 20-minute journey. These offences would range from using mobile phones while driving, speeding, red light running, to failing to indicate when changing lanes. Without the concept of discretion, I would never get to work! This chapter re-considers the fundamental role of uniformed police officers: is it pursuing the public interest or enforcing the law?

The idea of policing

The idea of policing, as we now know it, germinated out of the social turmoil of the industrial revolution in Great Britain and Ireland. This idea was championed by Sir Robert Peel, first as Secretary for Ireland and then as Home Secretary.[1] Peel established the Royal Irish Constabulary in 1822 and the Metropolitan Police in London in 1829. These organisations were to be uniformed and identifiable forces to control crime and maintain social order.[2]

Colonial governments, Queensland included, adopted the Irish model, it being best suited for controlling what could be considered a disengaged and defiant community. The Moreton Bay Convict Settlement was closed in 1835 and only opened to free settlement in 1842. The population of the Colony of Queensland of 1859 was still firmly rooted in its convict past, together with a growing immigrant community including significant numbers from Ireland.[3]

In addition, as European settlement expanded and displaced Aboriginal and Torres Strait Islanders, the original custodians of the land needed control, if not 'dispersal' (a euphemism at the time for indiscriminate killing). The Mounted Native Police were formed specifically for this purpose in 1848 initially in New South Wales and subsequently Queensland. The Queensland Police Force was established by the *Police Act* 1863 on the 1 January 1864, five years after the Colony of Queensland.[4]

The Irish model separated the police from the community. The police took responsibility from the community to deal with crime and disorder. The Queensland Police Force was empowered to impose the will of government on the community. This paramilitary identity could be characterised as an armed, barracked and separate force of control and, as described by Turner and his colleagues,[5] as an expression of the coercive power of government.[6]

By contrast, Peel's 'modern policing principles' formed the basis for London's Metropolitan Police. These principles focused on the philosophy of policing the community with their consent. The social and political opposition in England in the milieu of the French Revolution to the formation a police agency was significant. The police were seen a curtailing a free and liberal Britain. To achieve the required political acceptance of the idea of police required a model where acting in the public interest was central to police operations.[7] In contrast to the Irish-colonial model, the Metropolitan Police model could be characterised as being an unarmed force, living in the community and preventing crime through deterrence and minimum use of force. Turner's definition would characterise this as persuasive power.[8]

The history of policing in Queensland is firmly founded in the colonial adoption of the Irish model of coercive policing. Formal rejection of this model in Queensland did not come until the introduction of the *Police Service Administration Act* 1990[9] which adopted the community policing philosophy in the aftermath of the Fitzgerald Inquiry.[10]

Legislative basis of policing in Queensland and the public interest

The *Police Service Administration Act* 1990 *(PSAA),* and its predecessors the *Police Act* 1863 and *Police Act* 1936, are the formal instruments that expressed the will of the State of Queensland to create and maintain an agency for the enforcement of its laws and the keeping of peace and good order.[11] Unlike its predecessors, the *PSAA* in section 2.3 defines the functions of the Police Service as: the 'preservation of peace and good order in all areas in the State'; the protection of all communities and people from 'unlawful disruption of peace and good order'; the 'responsible, fair and efficient' administration of the law; and the 'rendering of such services' required of officers by the 'reasonable expectations of the community'.

The *PSAA* in section 2.4 outlines the community's responsibility for maintaining peace and good order, and that the Service is to 'act in partnership with the community at large to the extent compatible with efficient and proper performance' of its functions. The *PSAA* outlines the underpinning of the philosophy of the requirement for the QPS to seek out communities and establish what is their public interest in the delivery of police services.

The *PSAA* does not define who or what the 'community' is, nor does the *Acts Interpretation Act* 1954 (Queensland). The *Acts Interpretation Act* does, however, require words to be interpreted by their 'normal meaning'. So, what is the normal meaning of community? Tom Frame offers a definition of the 'public' as the 'shared life of the community'. He goes on to suggest a pluralistic construction of the 'public' that is diverse and diffuse and, in an Australian context, 'fragmented'.[12] In the Queensland context the public interest is not a single interest or public but a collective of communities whose interests vary geographically, economically and socially. The question for the Queensland Police Service (QPS) is to legitimately and fairly service these different and valid interests within its legislative and social mandate.

Uniquely in Queensland public sector enabling legislation, the *PSAA* defines and restricts the relationship between the Parliament, the Minister and the Commissioner for Police. In section 4.3 of the *PSAA* the conditions of appointment of the Commissioner are detailed and include the requirement of the minister to consult with and obtain the approval of the Chair of the Crime and Corruption Commission for this appointment. This is designed to circumvent politicisation of the Commissioner's appointment as occurred with the appointment of Commissioner Terry Lewis in 1977. Equally, section 4.5 of the *PSAA* outlines the conditions for the Commissioner's removal which also includes the requirement for a recommendation from the Chair of the Crime and Corruption Commission, or an 'address from the Legislative Assembly praying for the Commissioner's removal'.

Section 4.6 and 4.7 of the *PSAA* stipulate the recordings of all 'reports and recommendations' about the 'administration and functioning' of the police service between the Minister and Commissioner. The Minister, in turn, may give directions in writing to the Commissioner concerning the overall 'administration, management and superintendence' of the Police Service. These written directions must be published and placed before the Legislative Assembly.

These provisions are designed to ensure transparency in decision-making by both the Minister and the Commissioner, this transparency being a major component in demonstrating these players are acting in the public interest. They are supposed to ensure a degree of separation between the political will of the day and police operations. The reality is that few directions have ever come from the Minister in the 'prescribed' manner and for many years a report tabled in the Legislative Assembly has shown no complying directions have been made.

The Office of Constable and the Crown – the basis of discretion

As demonstrated by the provisions of the *PSAA*, the intent of the Queensland Parliament was to establish a clear separation between the political will of the day and its control over the operations of its coercive executive arm, the police. The intent was to cement this idea of the separation of ministerial and police powers in a clear and transparent way yet still ensure a legislative foundation for protection of what may be the public interest.

There is also a broader legal concept at play within the police context. The idea in common law of the Crown and the Office of Constable. These common law rights and responsibilities of the office of constable were recently confirmed in Queensland in a Queensland Court of Appeal decision, *Nugent v Stewart (Commissioner of Police) & Anor* [2016] QCA 223.[13] As part of the Commissioner's conditions of appointment under section 4.3 of the *PSAA*, the Commissioner's employment is said to be by the Crown. Similarly, appointments of Executive Officers (section 5.4) are said to be by the Crown. Commissioned officers, non-commissioned officers and constables have and exercise all powers and duties of a constable at common law (section 3.2).

Police employment by the Crown is coupled with the concept at common law of the Office of Constable. The basis for the Office of Constable is set out in the traditional oath or affirmation taken by constables upon appoint-ment. The wording of this Oath has remained fundamentally unchanged in Queensland (and elsewhere in the Commonwealth) since 1863. The oath requires allegiance to serve the monarch 'without favour or affection, malice or ill will' to keep and preserve the Queen's peace and 'prevent all offences against the same'.[14]

It is on this legal basis that police act as independent agents of the Crown, rather than through the delegated legislative authority of a public servant. This allows police discretion of action and in the enforcement of the law. It also sets the preservation of the 'peace' above simply enforcing of law. It could be argued that public servants do not have this legal discretion not to enforce a law as they are required to act in accordance with that law through a delegated responsibility rather than as a discretionary agent of the Crown. A standard legal definition of the Crown is the 'whole legal edifice of execu-tive government'.[15]

Toward a definition of the public interest and the Queen's peace

In policing, what is the Queen's peace and how is the public interest served by its preservation? Does the exercise of discretion in the enforcement of the law override the public interest expressed through the will of the parliament?

Uhr discusses the dichotomy of the provision of public leadership to a disparate public.[16] This discussion centred on the difficulty of who has the voice of the public, which voice should be listened to and how do public leaders listen. The diverse nature of Queensland means the effects of a law or policy has very different effects on different communities. For example, courts have been critical of police for enforcing minor elements of the law at the price of causing a riot or, in extreme cases, death or both. There was a riot on Palm Island after an Indigenous man died in custody.[17]

Discretionary application of the law by police is seen as critical to achiev-ing the overriding public interest of peace and good order. Misuse of police discretion has also been at the heart of police corruption. The Fitzgerald Inquiry into corruption, conducted between 1987 and 1989, was initially established to examine the policing of prostitution and illegal gambling. The public and government of the day were not only tolerant of this corruption but, in many ways, complicit in its persistence.[18]

The police regulated rather than eradicated these illegal activities. It was a failure at all levels of public leadership, either through self-delusion or a culture of permissiveness, that allowed corruption to extend beyond police to become integral to the fabric of public life in Queensland. Hence, the Fitzgerald Inquiry was about much more than crime and its prevention, it was about culture and its renewal. The critical outcomes of the inquiry were about changing the mood and mindset of public leaders, including among those holding public office.

In Queensland, the parliament, the press and the people acknowledged the traditional role of police as an 'invisible hand', acting as social agents to preserve the kind of peace that would allow the community to function socially and economically. Police perform this function through a social contract with the community they serve and from which they derive authority to function. Fundamental to this social contract is the legitimacy of the police in the broader community as the ultimate enforcer of the public interest expressed through the government and the law. Legitimacy is reliant on the community's trust in the police to act with equity, fairness, reasonableness, transparency and justice. In commercial terms, legitimacy is the value of the police 'brand' and, in accounting terminology, as the worth of its 'goodwill'. But what must the police do when the public interest is unclear or when the political message from both a national and state perspective is confused or, at best, unclear? How do police, as public leaders, discern which is the legitimate voice of the public interest, especially when those interests become more diverse?

Policing the conduct of anti-coal protests will serve to illustrate my point. Politically, there are contradictions about climate policy and support of the coal industry although there is a strong economic need to ensure the continuation of the coal industry. If the coal industry is fundamentally bad for the planet, the nation and its future, and that future is not supported by different elements of the government, how are protests against this apparent social wrong that brings in billions of dollars royalty revenue and economic benefit to be policed?

The question of public interest has been starkly illustrated by the media reaction to recent police action against foreign journalists covering a coal protest. Whose public interest do these journalists represent? Are their national and journalistic interests something that Queensland police should consider within the context of the Queensland community's public interest. Who wants to be the police commander of a protest that ends in the first climate martyr?

Community engagement – discerning the public interest

In addition to the legislative and parliamentary accountabilities of ministerial responsibility and reporting, the QPS has several strategies designed to draw out and engage with communities. The 2017–2021 strategic plan requires the fostering of 'collaborative partnerships with government agencies, non-government organisations, and community groups to maximise community safety'.[19]

The nature of the business of the QPS is concerned with connecting with community and partnering with communities in reducing the impact of crime and disorder. The QPS mission and vision statements emphasise both partnership with the community and building relationships. The QPS objectives include the 'supporting ... building safe, caring and connected communities by ... collaborating and consulting with all sectors of the community'.[20]

The QPS major risk statement 2017–2018 includes 'a reduction in community confidence and engagement with police'. The 2017–2018 outlook statement includes the sustaining of 'the support and cooperation of the community to work in partnership', emphasising both positive and negative requirements of community engagement, maintaining legitimacy and community confidence. The QPS Annual Report outlines these partnerships to include other government agencies and community partnerships through the establishment of community police boards in each of police district, Queensland Police Citizens Youth Welfare Association with their network of community-based clubs throughout Queensland, Neighbourhood Watch Queensland, Crime Stoppers Queensland and Volunteers in Policing.[21]

Policing services in Queensland are also delivered in nearly every population centre through 335 local police stations and 92 residential police beats and shopfronts. In a significant number of towns, the police are the only real presence of the government in those communities, such as McKinley, Pentland and Kynuna. This answers Frame's question about the capacity of government to reach out to diverse communities. The QPS is that presence and part of the great diversity that are the people in Queensland.[22] This emphasis on partnership and connectedness is reflected in several QPS corporate documents including, for example, the QPS Client Service Charter, QPS Aboriginal and Torres Strait Islander Strategic Directions 2015–2019, Queensland Counter Terrorism Strategy 2013–2018, and the Code of Conduct.[23]

In the virtual sense the QPS also maintains a substantial community outreach through its social media presence. For example, the QPS Facebook site has more than 860,000 followers and is liked by over 913,000 people. The QPS has used its Facebook page as a tool for delivering its corporate messages directly to this diverse group of users. It has used its social media accounts as a means to get real time feedback from the community about crime and other events. The QPS has also established a number of locally based community blog sites as well and is now piloting locally authored Facebook sites.

In practical terms, how do police reconcile all this garnered community interest. For example, a community whose local economy is dependent on the coal industry, and the climate change protester's interest in planetary survival? Which is paramount? Or do the police simply enforce the law using the 1899 Criminal Code, an expression of the will of a long-gone parliament?

Measuring success in meeting the public interest

As discussed above much of the business of the QPS is concerned with connecting with the community and partnering with these communities in reducing the impact of crime. As outlined in Peel's ninth principle of policing, 'the test of police efficiency is the absence of crime and disorder, not the visible evidence of police action in dealing with them.'[24]

The primary means of measuring success are qualitative measures such as 'Queenslander confidence in the police', 'Queenslanders were satisfied with their most recent contact with police', and the rate of complaints against police action. Certainly, police action against crime is also an important factor in maintaining public confidence but success is measured in 'feelings' of safety rather than in the statistics of crime and clear up rates.

If the primary goal of police is the maintenance of a peaceful community, then the real test is the absence of disorder and the measure, even more nebulously, is peace and prosperity.

Endnotes

1   RW Johnston, *The Long Blue Line*, Boolarong, Brisbane, 1992.
2   M Finnane, *Police and Government Histories of Policing in Australia*, Oxford University Press, Melbourne, 1994.
3   Johnston, *The Long Blue Line*; R Fitzgerald, L Megarrity and D Symons, *Made In Queensland: A New History*, UQ Press, Brisbane, 2009, pp. 13–17.
4   Fitzgerald et al, *Made In Queensland*, pp. 13–17.
5   Paul t'Hart & John Uhr (eds), *Public Leadership; Perspective and Practices*, ANU E-Press, Canberra, 2008, pp. 66–68.
6   M Finnane, *Policing in Australia Historical Perspectives*. 1987, UNSW Press, Sydney, 1987, p. 28.
7   Finnane, *Police and Government Histories of Policing in Australia*.
8   t'Hart & Uhr, *Public Leadership*.
9   *Police Service Administration Act* 1990 (Qld).
10 *Commission of Inquiry into Possible Illegal Activities and Associated Police Misconduct, Report of a Commission of Inquiry Pursuant to Orders in Council dated (i) 26 May 1987 (ii)24 June 1987 (iii) 25 August 1988 (iv) 29 June 1989*. 1989: Brisbane, p. 230–236; Queensland Legislative Assembly, *Votes and Proceedings 20 March 1990*, 1990, Queensland Hansard, p. 449–459.
11 *Police Act* 1936, Queensland.
12 Tom Frame, *Public Leadership: A Commentary*, UNSW, Canberra, 2018, pp. 4–5.
13 *Nugent v Stewart (Commissioner of Police) & Another*, Queensland Court of Appeal, 2016, p. 223.
14 *Police Act* 1863 (Qld); *Police Service Administration Act* 1990 (Qld); *Police Act* 1936 (Qld).
15 *Butterworth's Concise Australian Legal Dictionary*, Third Edition, LexisNexis, Sydney, 2004, p. 107.
16 t'Hart & Uhr, *Public Leadership*, pp. 66–68.
17 *Wotton v State of Queensland (No5)[2016] FCA 1457*, Federal Court of Australia, 2016, p. 1457.
18 *Commission of Inquiry into Possible Illegal Activities and Associated Police Misconduct, Report of a Commission of Inquiry Pursuant to Orders in Council dated (i) 26 May 1987 (ii)24 June 1987 (iii) 25 August 1988 (iv) 29 June 1989*, Brisbane, 1989, pp. 230–236.
19 *Queensland Police Service Strategic Plan 2017–2021*, Queensland Police Service, Brisbane.
20 *Queensland Police Service Strategic Plan 2017–2021*, Queensland Police Service, Brisbane.
21 *Queensland Police Service Strategic Plan 2017–2021*, Queensland Police Service, Brisbane.
22 *Queensland Police Service Annual Report 2016–2017*, Queensland Police Service, Brisbane.

23 *Queensland Police Service Client Service Charter; Queensland Police Service Aboriginal and Torres Strait Islander Strategic Directions 2015–2019; Queensland Counter Terrorism Startegy 2013–2018.*

24 JM Brown (ed.), *The Future of Policing*, Routledge, Abingdon, 2014.

CHAPTER 11

Philosophical tension and the public interest: the case of the NDIS

Simon Joyce

P rogram delivery for government is becoming more complex, more multidisciplinary, and more nuanced as the expectations of the broader public of government increase. These increasing complexities are the subject of the current review into the public service by David Theody. They will not be addressed as a focal point in this chapter. Program delivery, as an expression of the public interest becomes progressively more challenging as the size and scalability of a reform, or a program, increases. It is the potential for this to be in conflict with the underlying philosophy of a program that is focus of this chapter.

To look at the practical effect of this, the chapter will look at the philosophical tension between implementation of programs, and use the National Disability Insurance Scheme (NDIS) as a contemporary example of a program which experiences a philosophical tension in the delivery of a program. It will look at the philosophical tension between a participant's ability to have autonomy over their funding package, choose supports that meet their needs, and achieve goals associated with social and economic participation, and balance this with the needs of government and public servants to manage public monies and the resources of government effectively, ethically, and efficiently.

For clarity, this chapter does not reflect the opinion of, or views of, government, the public sector, or organisations directly linked to the rollout of the NDIS. This chapter should not be linked to any particular organisation, government body, or individual, and is an academic exploration of the tension between philosophy and delivery. It will not make commentary on the merits of a particular program or its delivery. It will look at the challenges in balancing these philosophical tensions only, and its relationship to the public interest more broadly.

The National Disability Insurance Scheme

The NDIS is the biggest reform undertaken by Australian governments in recent memory. While it is showcased as a significant social reform, the NDIS extends well beyond the parameters of a social reform. It is also a significant economic reform. It represents an investment by government in the lives of all Australians, and in the economy, providing a significant level of economic stimulus as a by-product of the delivery of the scheme. The NDIS will pump around $22 billion dollars into the economy annually at maturity, and provides people with disability the opportunity to secure the supports they need to participate in the workforce, return to the workforce, or contribute to the economy in a manner of their choosing.

When the Productivity Commission released its report into the state of disability care and support in Australia in 2011, it painted a grand picture of universal coverage for Australians who are born with, or acquire during their lifetime, a permanent disability.[1] It identified the deficiencies within the existing frameworks and schemes delivered by the states and territories, and what should be done to address these. One of its key findings was that:

> There should be a new national scheme – the National Disability Insurance Scheme (NDIS) – that provides insurance cover for all Australians in the event of significant disability. Funding of the scheme should be a core function of government (just like Medicare).[2]

In 2013 the Australian Parliament enacted the scheme through the *National Disability Insurance Scheme Act 2013*, and established the National Disability Insurance Agency (NDIA) as a Corporate Commonwealth Entity, with a board, and a CEO, with the mandate to implement the scheme over the coming years.[3] Establishment of the scheme, and the NDIA to administer it, marked the beginning of the delivery phase of the reform. People with disability would be able to receive a plan, with funded supports which would support them to achieve their goals.

An argument could be made that the NDIS is an instrument of the public interest. This is reflected in the current operational model, with a combination of people to guide participants through the pathway. This includes internal planners who hold delegated powers under the Act to approve plans for participants. Agency planners are complemented by the partners in community program which supports participants through the participant pathway. This holistic approach to the pathway is designed to support participants navigate the scheme.

Governments have a number of levers that they can utilise in order to deliver on this concept of the public interest. They can propose legislation, they can regulate, they can create policies, and they can design programs. The quintessence of successful program design is focussed around the impact on an end user, or recipient of a program, and managing potential philosophical conflicts which can arise in the delivery of programs.

The NDIS philosophy

At its core, the scheme is aspirational. The scheme's principles presume a close relationship between the public interest and the NDIS. The multidisciplinary and multifaceted program has key altruistic and practical pillars. A program which will change the lives of hundreds of thousands of Australians living with a disability surely has to be a practical example of government acting in the public interest.

The current planning focus is determining the goals for a participant and crafting a statement of supports, or a plan around them, which will help to achieve these goals. This is a practical reflection of the scheme's philosophy. The scheme is not just about the provision of supports nor about how much money is in a plan. It is about facilitating the ability for people with disability to achieve their goals and aspiration. This philosophy of empowerment, and choice, underpins the scheme. It is a reflection of the approach taken in the scheme's establishment to deliver choice and control to people with disability.

The fundamental philosophy which guides the scheme is based on the UN Convention on the Rights of Persons with Disabilities. This philosophy of autonomy and empowerment even feeds into selection and assessment decisions in recruitment activities for staff who look to join the NDIA. One of the core selection criteria in recruitment has been contemporary attitudes to disability. The focus of having this as a core criterion brings people into the Agency administering the scheme who have positive approaches, and lived experience with disability.

The NDIS philosophy and contemporary attitudes to disability are primarily focussed on enablement and empowerment. People are empowered to make decisions about their destiny and their autonomy, and this is enabled by appropriate engagement and navigable interfaces with government. Program design caters for philosophy to be expressed through a programs delivery. It is during the delivery phase where a programs philosophical tensions can arise. This is particularly true of social programs with a human centred focus.

The tension between philosophy and program delivery

Philosophical tension between the ethos of programs and the delivery of programs is not a new concept, albeit it is more pronounced in recent times. In fact, the Australian public service has looked at how complicated program delivery, and how complicated policy development, can be addressed in the modern environment. The APS did this through the 2012 publication, *Tackling Wicked Problems: a public policy perspective.*[4] These challenges are faced by senior leaders in the modern public sector and in ever increasing examples of complicated multidisciplinary services delivery.

The tension for the NDIS is the difference between the philosophy of empowerment, and enablement, and the requirement to manage public monies judiciously. The challenge is how to balance the needs of participants for the choice and control that is critical to the ethos underpinning the scheme, with the requirements that are imposed on officials in the administration of public monies, ensuring strong regulatory and compliance frameworks, and the delivery of effective programs. The public interest is most effectively served by strong programs that reflect community expectations delivered by public officials who know the law and the latitude given to them within it.

In most areas of the 'commentariat', the approach to evaluating this tension is fragmented, focussing either on the delivery of supports, sustainability or funding viability. Put simply, the 'commentariat' and the media concentrate on one aspect of this tension and not on the balance. The focus will usually be on the outcomes for a participant, or a decision that has been made by an official within the governance and accountability frameworks for government. These assessments of the 'commentariat' avoid considering the broader strategic context in delivering programs which advance or support the public interest. Balancing these out, and exposing this tension, is something which academics, professionals, and members of the commentariat alike need to consider actively when expressing their views in any public forum.

Noting the scope of this program, it is no surprise that the expenditure of Commonwealth funds is subject to intense scrutiny in the media, through parliamentary committees, and by advocates in the community. Exploration of the performance of the Agency through an analysis of its operational activities, effectively feeds into the interests of the public. While this does not mean it is necessarily congruent with the public interest, it supports the principles of efficient and ethical management of resources allocated for delivery of the scheme.

So how do program administrators strike the right balance between philosophy, practicality and program delivery? If there was no regulation governing the provision of services, and supports, the scheme would run out of money. Similarly, looking only on a rigid set of participation or support criteria that is expressed in a way that does not attend closely to the individual nuances of disability, especially functional impairment, would only lead to a cookie-cutter model that merely reflected the old way of doing things which is funding organisations to deliver services on an industrial scale. Who is responsible for striking that balance between philosophy and pragmatic delivery? Finding the balance is simply trying to identify the public interest. The public interest is served by a program that delivers outcomes, that manages public funds effectively and efficiently, ensuring optimal support for people with disabiltiies and value for money for taxpayers.

Where, then, does the responsibility rest? The legislature, the executive, the administrative arm of government? Is there a balance to be found across all these groups? I propose a narrower focus by coming to the centre of the scheme's intent, and delivery methodology. Delivery of the NDIS is through instruments known as plans, which provide a statement of funded supports available to the individual with a disability, who are given access to the scheme. Criteria for the development of these plans and this statement of supports are codified in Section 34 of the Act. These are essentially the rules which a delegate or planner must follow in assessing if supports are reasonable and necessary and should be included in a participant's support plan. These powers under the legislation are delegated to Agency officials who are accountable for development and approval of plans.

It is this delegate who makes the determination on whether or not supports should be included or not included within a plan who has to cast this balance. They are charged with making decisions that align with the legislation, community expectations, and the overall ethos of the scheme. It is not an easy task to undertake. A decision-maker has to balance their own judgment along with the regulatory framework within which they operate. In the case of the NDIS, the decision-maker determines what supports a participant will have in their lives, fully funded, to support meeting their goals. It is an extremely important responsibility, and not one a decision-maker can take lightly.

If we are looking at this purely through the prism of the intangible public interest, the legislation is not prescriptive. In contrast to some other legislative frameworks it is actually deficient when it comes to the public interest. Taking a literal view of the NDIS Act, there is only one mention of the public interest and it appears in section 66. This section of the legislation allows the CEO to disclose information when 'the CEO certifies that it is necessary in the public interest to do so.'[5] The remainder of the NDIS Act does not actually identify what this concept of the public interest is in the context of the NDIS. But a common sense approach would be that the benefits of an NDIS as identified in the original Productivity Commission report must be in the public interest. It would be counterintuitive to argue that a scheme which gives autonomy, choice and control to participants would not be in the public interest. If it is, therefore, in the public interest, then what does that mean for this tension between its philosophy and its program delivery? If administrative decision-making tells us anything, it is that every consideration has a relative or absolute weight. Is it the philosophy, the vision of the programs creators, or the pragmatic approach taken in implementing it which carries the greatest weight in this discussion?

While defining the public interest, stewardship of the public interest, and delivering on the public interest may indeed be the purview of elected representatives, implementation or operationalisation of these programs within that conceptual framework can present practical challenges for officials. Officials deliver the program of work of the government of the day, in a way free from bias, and in a way that is consistent with the APS Values. But where officials are exercising decision-making powers in the course of their duty and, indeed, rolling out programs such as the NDIS, this tension between philosophy and program delivery can easily arise.

Delegates, as they undertake their duties, must be conscious of 'reasonable and necessary' supports. The concept of 'reasonable and necessary' is not a new one. The judiciary has this concept already embedded within it, the reasonable person test. Both practically and philosophically, this presents a tension, between the ethos of the scheme, social and economic participation for people with disability through choice and control over their supports, with the prescription of controls associated with the expenditure of government money.

Another philosophical tension overlays the practicalities of the NDIS, and whether it is a reform which is in the public interest as a tool of social and economic engineering: that of sustainability. The scheme provides universal cover, but not everyone can access it. In order to participate, the scheme needs to assess if you are eligible for support. This is where a key tension comes into focus. There are more people with disability in Australia than those that were forecast to be originally funded under the scheme. More than 400,000 individuals will eventually be given access to the scheme. But there will be other individuals with a disability who will not be eligible or they will be unable to get the supports they want or prefer. This, too, is not a new feature in government programs. Part of a vigorous democratic debate is to highlight where programs fail or where programs succeed.

Design of the NDIS is contingent on use of other enabling service programs to provide the supports for people within the community. Empowering communities, and building supports in these communities, builds capacity, capability, and resilience. Investing in communities pays dividends through ensuring that some of the most vulnerable members of our communities are provided with the services to achieve their goals and aspirations. There are different ways to administer the NDIS and its implementation that will manage the enduring tension between organisational philosophy and program delivery. Information Linkages and Capacity Building (ILC) grants are one approach but many other tools are available.

Perhaps remarkably, the presence of the ILC Program within the broader NDIS framework actually works to ease the philosophical tension between the two camps. This may be because programs delivered through grant agreements instead of other payment mechanisms tend to have more flexibility in delivery models than other funding and payment models. The ILC program builds the capacity, willingness and capability of communities to provide informal supports, as well as better connecting participants with mainstream services.

It is difficult to envision a circumstance where a successfully delivered NDIS is not in the public interest. With such a human-centred focus on the delivery of the scheme, and the benefits realised with an emphasis on early intervention and capacity building, there is a clear link to delivering public value. While something may be entirely in the public interest, I could simultaneously put forward the view that a policy, or program, only delivers on the public interest through successful leadership of the reform's implementation. As with so much public administration, leadership is a key factor in ensuring efficient operations and achieving effective outcomes.

Resolving philosophical tension

In the expectation-charged environment in which the NDIS operates, there is likely to be a significant disconnect between community expectations and what the scheme can actually deliver. Contrary to popular belief, significant public sector reforms involving very substantial sums of public money take time to implement and validate. These reforms need to be well-considered and carefully managed. Consistent with many areas of public policy, the context is never static. Governments have changing priorities and ministers, who bring an emphasis of their own, come and go. A commitment to identifying and then pursuing the public interest requires insightful leadership and gifted management. It draws on personal experience and collective expertise.

There is an expectation that senior leaders, including the Senior Executive Service (SES), will advance the public interest by delivering whole-of-government leadership, particularly the delivery of multimodal programs such as the NDIS. These expectations are set out in section 35 of the *Public Service Act*.

> The function of the SES is to provide APSwide strategic leadership of the highest quality that contributes to an effective and cohesive APS. For the purpose of carrying out the function of the SES, each SES employee:
>
> a. provides one or more of the following at a high level: (i) professional or specialist expertise; (ii) policy advice; (iii) program or service delivery; (iv) regulatory administration; and
>
> b. promotes cooperation within and between Agencies, including to deliver outcomes across Agency and portfolio boundaries; and
>
> c. by personal example and other appropriate means, promotes the APS Values, the APS Employment Principles and compliance with the Code of Conduct.

Plainly, officials are held to a higher standard of public scrutiny because they are handling public money and, in the case of the NDIS, very large sums.

Public leadership is not, then, so much a solution to the underlying tension but, when delivered effectively, acts as a management control for this tension. Leadership is the underlying means available to individuals who are advancing the public interest in managing these competing interests and tensions and, indeed, the other challenges associated with program delivery. Without strong public leadership, then the ability to manage the philosophical tension effectively is diminished, and ultimately means that unintended outcomes may arise in delivery of the program.

For complex, multimodal, and multidisciplinary delivery of programs whether in the public or the private sector, it is essential to ensure that leaders consider the philosophical tension that can arise in program delivery and ensure that the tension is effectively addressed. The exercise of such leadership remains a challenge not just for the APS executives but for the political community as well – the nation's elected representatives and those who advise them.

Endnotes

1   Productivity Commission 2011, *Disability Care and Support*, Report no. 54, Canberra.
2   Productivity Commission 2011, *Disability Care and Support*, Report no. 54, Canberra, p. 2.
3   Commonwealth of Australia, *National Disability Insurance Scheme Act* 2013 (as amended), Compilation No. 9, 1 July 2018, Office of Parliamentary Counsel, Canberra.
4   Australian Public Service Commission (2012), 'Tackling wicked problems: a public policy perspective', http://www.apsc.gov.au/publications-and-media/archive/ publications-archive/tackling-wicked-problems.
5   Commonwealth of Australia, *National Disability Insurance Scheme Act* 2013 (as amended), Compilation No. 9, 1 July 2018, Office of Parliamentary Counsel, Canberra.

CHAPTER 12

Managing water in the Murray-Darling Basin

Wendy Craik

I was asked in 2018 to review the findings of eight reports and inquiries related to alleged theft of water from the Barwon-Darling catchment in the Murray-Darling Basin.[1] Predictably, the reports were in measured language. For example Ken Matthews' report had a clear message, 'no meter no pump'.[2] The language in the submissions to the parallel Senate Inquiry into the water market was a different matter.[3] It revealed a flood of distressed, angry, frustrated complaints questioning the integrity of water management in the Murray-Darling Basin, alleging that some governments were bending the rules in favour of irrigation, failing to protect environmental water, designing rules to undermine the Basin Plan and failing to ensure compliance with the agreed measures in place. While I am not saying these allegations are true, I was shocked by the vehemence and consistency of these statements.

One of the roles of government is to manage inherent self-interest in human behaviour towards delivering the public interest. Adam Smith said that 'every individual … neither intends to promote the public interest, nor knows how much he is promoting it, he intends only his own gain'.[4] These sentiments are akin to Garrett Hardin's 'tragedy of the commons' in that, in the absence of government action, 'users act in self interest contrary to the common good depleting and spoiling a resource through their collective action'.[5] This is unless, as Elinor Ostrom pointed out, property rights and other management arrangements have been agreed and implemented by the users of the resource.[6]

It is usually relatively obvious when the public interest is not being met in the exploitation of a natural resource but it is less straightforward to determine when it is being met consistent with the agreed objective. In the case of the Murray-Darling Basin, the objective of the 2007 Commonwealth *Water Act* is to manage the Murray-Darling Basin water resources in the public interest. The legislation includes giving effect to relevant international agreements, ensuring sustainable extraction, protecting and restoring ecological values and ecosystem services, optimising economic, social and environmental outcomes and maximising net economic returns.[7]

How the totality of those objects is implemented is challenging and there is considerable disagreement about their interpretation as illustrated by the deliberations of the Royal Commission in South Australia.[8] These objects are not, however, dissimilar to objects of other Acts which relate to management of other natural resources, although the *Water Act* has rather a large number of specific objects.

A process of public consultation is the usual government approach to ensuring the public interest objects of natural resource management legislation are met. Such a consultation commonly begins with a management plan that spells out the vision and the objectives; the resource will then be described; the principles for resource allocation will be listed; and finally, the science, the economics and cultural values on which the allocation is based will be articulated. A draft is usually put out for further public consultation prior to the development of what becomes the final version. This form of words may require legislative approval.

Once the plan is adopted, a good practice is that a compliance regime is established, monitoring of the resource and its uses is undertaken and reported to the community. Sanctions related to the egregiousness of any infringement are applied, a means of conflict resolution is usually established and the plan is adapted over time to ensure it remains effective and consistent with contemporary science, economics and culture.

The Murray-Darling Basin Plan became law in 2012. In formal terms:

> It is the legal framework to reset the balance of water use in the Basin.
> It sets environmental and other objectives for the Basin and establishes
> new, lower sustainable extraction limits to achieve them. It also outlines

the key actions, processes and timeframes that Governments are to adopt to implement the Plan.[9]

Like most major natural resource management arrangements that cover multiple jurisdictions and attempt to meet multiple objectives, the Plan is the culmination of trade-offs between environmental, economic and social matters. The values assigned to these parameters often depends on the point of view of the proposer and change with time, science and community expectations. For example, in the Great Barrier Reef Marine Park, the scientific community in the late 1980s regarded setting aside some five percent of park area for non-extractive activity as appropriate. By the time the Marine Park was re-zoned in 2003, the scientists regarded the appropriate area to be set aside for non extractive activity to be 30 percent of park area.

As has been painfully evident, the Murray-Darling Basin Plan has been contentious with multiple objectives, users, jurisdictions and perspectives. Severe and continuing drought and the effects of climate change are exacerbating tensions and inflaming irreconcilable debates between those demanding more water for irrigators or more water for the environment or more water for communities. The alleged water theft in the northern Basin, accusations of many millions of dollars of government money funding extensive and inappropriate irrigation infrastructure, multiple massive fish deaths in the Darling River and communities running out of water have been accompanied by trenchant criticism that the Basin is not being managed in the public interest.

A major issue in some of these debates is the inability of the community to judge the state of the water resource beyond the headline public statements, whether it is improving or deteriorating, and what action is required to bring it to a state in which the community will be reassured that it is being well managed. In the absence of transparent, complete and credible reporting of relevant water information, it is not surprising that the community believes the worst, whether the reporting is true or not.

Twenty years ago Australian fisheries resources were the subject of significant criticism and heated debate about their condition and management. I recall unpleasant meetings, fishers suffering severe financial hardship and occasional threats of violence. While there were reports on the state of fisheries, they did not routinely and readily demonstrate the state of the fishery for the community or the fishers or what would be the appropriate action given the state of the resource. Over a period of years a standardised system of reporting the state of Australian fisheries stocks has been developed and the 2018 version is now available via a smartphone. The 'Status of Australian Fish Stocks' (SAFS) provides a ready reference as to how 120 Australian fish species made up of 406 stocks are faring.[10] Drafting SAFS involves all jurisdictions and is facilitated by the Fisheries Research and Development Corporation. SAFS classes stocks according to their classification across a consistent framework which is related to fishery stock status ranging from negligible, progressing through undefined, depleted, recovering, depleting to sustainable. The reports now cover the majority of Australian-caught fish that Australians will eat. Of those stocks, 254 are classified as sustainable.

Table 1 (below) illustrates the kind of synthesised information available and demonstrates how easy it is to grasp the status of a particular stock or species.[11] SAFS is produced every two years and the 2018 version involved 100 fishery scientists (from fisheries agencies, CSIRO and universities) working together translating the stock assessments undertaken for jurisdictions into the framework outlined above. The work of these scientists is then independently peer-reviewed by another 50 scientists before it is finalised. Essential elements of the success of SAFS have been the gradual development and refinement of the process, independent peer reviews of the work and detailed archiving of all records, reviews and versions.[12]

This process (and no doubt other processes, such as harvest strategies and buybacks) have, in my view, resulted in Australian fisheries being a much less contentious area of debate than previously. There is not the argument of old about the management of the various fishery resources now that this process has been put in place. Contrast this with the level of disputation on the effects of water plans and levels of extractions in the Murray-Darling Basin.

Providing a useful basis for completer water accounts is the independent assessment of resources by the Bureau of Meteorology's (BOM) assumption of responsibility for issuing national water information standards, collecting and publishing water information, conducting regular national water resources assessments, publishing an annual National Water Account, providing regular water availability forecasts giving advice on matters relating to water

Table 1. Examples of stock status changes 2014–2018

SPECIES	2014 Stock status	2016 Stock status	2018 Stock status
Blacklip Abalone			
Victorian Central Zone Fishery	Depleted	Depleting	Depleting
New South Wales	Recovering	Sustainable	Depleting
Victorian Western Zone Fishery	Depleted	Sustainable	Sustainable
Tasmanian Eastern Zone Fishery	Recovering	Sustainable	Depleting
Blue Swimmer Crab			
Cockburn Sound	Depleted	Depleted	Recovering
Shark Bay	Depleted	Recovering	Recovering
Gulf St Vincent	Recovering	Sustainable	Sustainable
Snapper			
West coast	Recovering	Recovering	Recovering
Shark Bay inshore —Freycinet Estuary	Recovering	Sustainable	Sustainable
Ballot Saucer Scallop			
Ballot's Saucer Scallop Abrolhos Islands and Mid-West Trawl Managed Fishery	Depleted	Depleted	Sustainable
Shark Bay Scallop Managed Fishery	Depleted	Recovering	Sustainable
Black Jewfish			
Northern Territory	Depleted	Depleted	Recovering

information and enhancing understanding of Australia's water resources.[13] The process of reporting in the National Water Account is transparent and builds confidence and understanding in the volumes published regarding water traded, extracted for use, recovered and managed for economic, public and environmental purposes. Prior to the Bureau being given responsibility for this reporting, the information was provided by the states and therefore was subject to different modelling, approaches, resources and levels of precision. Since the Bureau has assumed responsibility there is not the disputation or doubt about the information that is produced.

The Bureau works with Commonwealth, state and territory government water agencies and utilities to produce the National Water Account. According to Grafton and Williams, New South Wales is a leader in implementing General Purpose Water Accounting Reports (GPWAR) that seek to provide consistent and transparent water information to all.[14] Despite acknowledging the significant commitments made by jurisdictions to implement the Murray-Darling Basin Compliance Compact which commits them to, among other things, a risk-based rollout of metering, timely information on diversions, environmental watering and ministerial decisions on water use, there are still gaps in the information available to the Bureau. These gaps include floodplain water use, private storage volumes and use, total diversions and uncertainties about climate change impacts. Following this paper's presentation in April 2019, Grafton and Williams suggested that, notwithstanding the progress made by the Bureau and jurisdictions, there is a need to identify and resolve gaps in knowledge and measurement of water in the Basin to provide comprehensive information on volumes in 'water storages (public and private), end of system flows, diversions, and return flows for all diversion categories by catchment'.[15] They also suggested chemical measures should be audited.

In other words, starting with the Bureau's accounts, Grafton and Williams propose that an independent audit of all Murray-Darling Basin water is required. Given the level of distrust and aggravation in the Basin, I am strongly inclined to agree that using the Bureau's accounts as the basis, an independent water audit should be undertaken. Further, it should be done annually. Were the auditor to categorise the confidence of water information, so that for each water resource plan area, assessments could show change over time in the quantity of take that is measured-versus-metered-versus-estimated, stakeholders and the community are more likely to have faith in what they are being told. There seems to be no good reason why water accounts should be treated differently from financial accounts, for which annual independent auditing is a routine matter and for which the absence of an independent audit would raise questions about the veracity of the accounts.

It is currently possible for almost any group purporting to represent the public interest to make a claim of outrage at some aspect of water management in the Basin and accuse another group of receiving favourable treatment under the Plan. Without an independent source of data to which to refer, these disputes are very likely to continue. I cannot help but contrast the drama surrounding water arrangements in the Basin with the relative silence that now envelops fisheries.

My view is that implementing an annual independent audit would go a long way to starting to reduce the level of distrust about water use and the degree to which the Murray-Darling Plan is delivering what has been promised. While there is still a long way to go with initiatives such as rolling-out timely measurement and reporting of all diversions, understanding how much is captured by private farm dams through an independent audit and detailed assessments of confidence in the information provided, would provide significantly greater transparency and accountability. This would lead to greater clarity in assessing progress on the delivery of the Basin Compliance Compact and accredited water resource plans, and hopefully lead to calmer debate and greater trust throughout the community that the Basin is being managed in the public interest.[16] Trust is crucial. Building trust is indispensable.

Endnotes

1   Wendy Craik, 'Murray-Darling Basin Compliance Compact', Report to COAG, 7 June 2018.
2   Ken Matthews, *Independent investigation into NSW water management and compliance: Interim Report,* 8 September 2017.
3   Senate Rural and Regional Affairs and Transport References Committee, *Inquiry into the integrity of the water market in the Murray-Darling Basin,* 2018.
4   Adam Smith, *The Theory of Moral Sentiments*, part IV, chap 1, 1759, pp. 184–85.
5   Garrett Hardin, 'Tragedy of the Commons', *Science,* new series, vol. 162, no. 3859, 13 December 1968, pp. 1243–48.
6   Elinor Ostrom, *Governing the Commons. The Evolution of Institutions for Collective Action*, Cambridge University Press, New York, 1990.
7   Commonwealth of Australia, *Water Act,* 2007, s 3.
8   Bret Walker, *Murray-Darling Basin Royal Commission Report,* 29 January 2019.
9   Productivity Commission, *Murray-Darling Basin: Five -Year Assessment,* Inquiry Report 2019, p. 4.
10 Annabel Boyer, 'Fish Stocks Update', *Fish*, vol. 27, no. 1, March 2019, pp. 10–11.
11 Annabel Boyer, 'Fish Stocks Update', *Fish*, vol 27, no. 1, March 2019, p. 10.
12 Carolyn Stewardson, FRDC, personal communication.
13 Bureau of Meteorology (BOM), *The National Water Account*, http://www.bom.gov.au/water/nwa/2018/mdb/index.shtml#, accessed 8 August 2019.
14 R Quentin Grafton and John Williams, 'Thirst for certainty: the urgent need for a water audit of the Murray-Darling Basin', *Farm Policy Journal*, vol. 16, no. 2, winter quarter 2019, pp. 14–22.
15 R Quentin Grafton and John Williams, 'Thirst for certainty: the urgent need for a water audit of the Murray-Darling Basin', *Farm Policy Journal*, vol. 16, no. 2, winter quarter 2019, p. 16.
16 Thanks to Megan Dyson and Neil Byron for their helpful comments on an earlier draft and to Tracey Arentz for her editorial assistance.

CHAPTER 13

Universities and the public interest

Tom Frame

This chapter examines the place of universities in Australian national life, whether they and their staff are required to serve the public interest and why attentiveness to the public interest is an effective operating principle.

Introduction

The importance of universities to the societies that host them has been assumed but barely even asserted for centuries. As a British settler society, establishing a university in the Colony of New South Wales was a sign of economic development and a symbol of social progress. The Act incorporating and endowing the University of Sydney in 1850 began with a statement of its objectives:

> Whereas it is deemed expedient for the better advancement of religion
> and morality and the promotion of useful knowledge, to hold forth to
> all classes and denominations of Her Majesty's subjects resident in the
> Colony of New South Wales, without any distinction whatsoever, an
> encouragement for pursuing a regular and liberal course of education …

Although the university was publicly financed, the legislation made no mention of the 'public interest' that would be served by the new establishment because the point and purpose of a university education was apparently accepted by the colony's leaders. Admittedly, it was rare for the public interest to be mentioned in nineteenth century legislation. Nonetheless, a civilised society needed educated people who would ensure the promotion of learning and the evolution of culture. This was a self-evident truth to those who authorised its funding.

By the time Australia became a Federal Commonwealth in 1901, the new nation hosted four universities: Sydney (1850), Melbourne (1853), Adelaide (1874) and Tasmania (1890). They were not large institutions by any measure. There were only 2,652 students, less than 0.1 percent of the population, and several hundred teaching staff. By 1939, the number of universities had increased to six with a student population of 14,236. Notably, 4,000 students were not seeking formal qualifications and a mere 81 were engaged in postgraduate research. After the Second World War and especially from the early 1970s when most professions required its members to have a bachelor's degree, the university population increased exponentially. In 2018, the higher education sector had 1,457,209 enrolled students of whom 1,066,073 were domestic students and 391,136 were international students. There were more than 600,000 Commonwealth-funded student places. In 2019, university activities are valued in excess of $30 billion per annum and the sector is considered vital to the nation's present prosperity and future well-being. But neither the growth of universities nor their contribution to the economy has translated into enduring community support or political goodwill.

In an address to the United Kingdom Universities Partnership Program in October 2017, the then Vice-Chancellor of Melbourne University, Professor Glyn Davis, noted the 'rising tide of hostility toward universities'.[1] He spoke of 'a rising chorus of complaints about arrogant universities that resist government priorities, that value research over teaching, that do not address community ambitions' and quoted higher education commentator Simon Marginson, Professor of Higher Education at Melbourne University, who asked: 'what greater good would be lost if universities closed tomorrow?'[2] He recalled the criticism of then Prime Minister Malcolm Turnbull that universities were paying too much attention to peer review and not enough to local industry. Marginson conceded that it was

> not hard to understand the frustration of elected politicians. Universities
> pay little tax yet are remorseless in asking for more public money. They

champion themselves as innovators yet resist political pressures for applied research and immediate impact ... hence the suspicion among politicians that ... universities have lost sight of real life.

As a concerned university administrator, Davis believed the best response was greater commitment to engagement by which he meant 'creating meaningful links between a university and its many constituencies, and communicating the fact that this is what we do'. But some forms of engagement were fraught with danger, such as that posed by

entrepreneurs offering bright, shiny alternatives, new ways of delivering education that promise to be cheaper, faster and essentially private. Ministers have motive. Silicon Valley provides the means. Creative destruction awaits. We ignore this at our peril.

Davis preferred 'building a stronger base in society – among graduates as among those who never attend university' with 'practical demonstrations of how teaching and research bring prosperity to the community, opportunities for the young, a richer and more engaged life for all'. Notably, he observed that engagement has '*quietly* found an institutional home in most universities, building links into community' [emphasis added].

There was no direct mention in his address of the responsibility of universities to serve the common good nor of the obligation of faculty to act in the public interest. Davis suggests that engagement – meaning intentional dialogue with community stakeholders presumably with the purpose of promoting public interests in a practical way – has come late to most Australian universities and something many consider a second order activity. This response partly reflects the force of institutional inertia and the prevalence of the dispersed mode of leadership encountered in many large organisations, the effects of personal preoccupation with disciplinary concerns among academics and a deficient understanding of the public interest that is commonly encountered among highly focussed individuals. While universities ought to acknowledge the messages coming from the societies that host them and upon whose goodwill they rely, there are compelling reasons for universities making advancement of the public interest an organising priority and an operating principle. And yet, reticence about doing so remains, with no Australian university having the phrase 'the public interest' featured in its charter.

The rise of the 'civic university'

The expectation that universities become more attentive to the public interest has provoked a more creative response in other parts of the world. A number of universities in Britain and Northern Europe have explored, and some have attempted to become, a new kind of institution – a 'civic' university – where the explicit institutional focus is pursuing the public interest. These universities have been motivated by a closer commitment to advancing the common good. Whereas academics have traditionally believed that the creation and dissemination of knowledge for its own sake would eventually bring benefits to society, relying largely on an 'invisible hand' to illuminate the connection, civic universities focus on the creation of new knowledge to address specific societal problems. They attempt to concentrate on the demand side of the knowledge exchange equation before turning their resources to the supply side, with an explicit link between society's grand challenges and their teaching and research agenda. The Vice-Chancellor of Newcastle University in the United Kingdom, Professor Chris Brink, contends that civic universities are different from their conventional counterparts in that responsiveness to societal need 'becomes an ambition in itself, and a driving force for academic work'. The civic university knows 'not only what it is good at but also what it is good for'.[3]

One of the main challenges for civic universities is the persistence of traditional performance indicators that have arguably worked to alienate universities from the public. In response to the existence of a widening gulf there has been a steady commitment to 'engagement' in university statements of strategic intent alongside the long-standing affirmation of teaching and research as the foremost scholarly activities. Several commentators contend that the 'un-civic university' sees these three pillars are distinct and even independent activities with engagement the least esteemed, often because it is hardest to measure. They note that the demarcation of teaching and research as separate modes of academic endeavour has largely dissolved in recent years because most scholars recognise they are overlapping and mutually enriching activities. Teaching becomes more relevant when linked to practical problems being considered by researchers, and research benefits from the development of applied coursework. But few academics appear convinced that incentives and investment, recognition and rewards for engagement activities are consistent with those associated with teaching and research. Engagement is what happens after institutional expectations of teaching and research performance have been met.

The self-styled civic universities have embraced what has been termed the 'quadruple helix' model of innovation enjoining the university, government, business and society. These universities take their lead from local, national and global affairs in deciding where to encourage the efforts of their staff and are transparent and accountable to their external stakeholders and the wider public for their performance in responding practically to societal problems. Such an approach to teaching and research is intended to destabilise and diminish the silos that have been erected by many academic disciplines, usually for their own professional ends, by obliging scholars to collaborate with their colleagues on practical problems that transcend traditional disciplinary boundaries.

The civic university also differs from the 'entrepreneurial university' – institutions whose courses meet market-driven student demand and whose research is derived from business partnerships – with its energies directed towards enterprise in both teaching and research. In the case of the teaching, the aim of the entrepreneurial university is attracting the largest number of students by offering courses shaped by employment imperatives and, in the case of research, funding activities that produce commercial returns particularly in the areas of national defence, health care and industrial efficiency. Conversely, the civic university is shaped by society and its needs and not by the market and its wants. There is, however, the challenge of identifying the individuals and institutions that represent or reliably relay the societal needs to which the civic university will respond.

Recent literature reveals three broad schools of thought and practice within the civic university model. These schools have been labelled social justice, economic sustainability and public good. The first school draws strongly on the political philosophy of John Rawls with an emphasis on the university's role in building stronger citizenship and more democratic societies. By encouraging greater participation in public life and eschewing the value-free perspective that purportedly characterises academic independence and scholarly integrity, the university is both cause and effect of social movements that are intended to improve everyday living for all people and not only those who can access an elite education. The social justice approach counters the 'knowledge for knowledge sake' approach that featured in Cardinal John Henry Newman's well-known but seldom-read 1852 essay *The Idea of a University.*

The economic sustainability approach is a polar opposite to the social justice approach in pursuing innovation and promoting technology as the means by which business and industry advance to the eventual benefit of the whole society. The university is committed to equipping the workforce and creating new opportunities for companies and corporations to enlarge the economic base, thereby increasing employment opportunities and living standards. This approach sees universities becoming 'state-subsidised entrepreneurs who exploit their academic capital in increasingly competitive situations' in the interests of private capital and public prosperity.[4] The university gives the state a clear competitive edge in a knowledge-driven economy and makes possible the kind of technological advance that addresses the social, economic and even political problems besetting a nation and its regional neighbours.

The public good (a hybrid term combining the common good and the public interest) approach is located between the two social justice and economic sustainability approaches. Because it is publicly funded, the university has a duty to contribute to the common good and promote the public interest. The public good approach is mindful that higher education can contribute to 'social benefit efficiency gains and potential equity effects on opportunity and reduced inequality'. Drawing on the seminal work of the American economist, Paul Samuelson, who developed the concept of a 'collective consumptive good' in 1954 – public goods produce benefits that are not easily divisible and can be enjoyed or consumed by everyone – knowledge is a public good because the benefits are indivisible and inexhaustible. The university is, therefore, a place of connection between the producers and consumers of knowledge in the state, business and civic sectors. The university serves as a venue for knowledge demands to be sifted and sorted according to a shared sense of the common good.

The difficulty facing a university seeking to embrace any of these approaches is the steady internationalisation and gradual commercialisation of the higher education sector. The first reflects the rise of a globalised labour market in which faculty pursue their academic vocation often with greater loyalty to their discipline than to an institution or a community. The second is a consequence of reduced government investment in higher education and the need to compete for overseas students who are often without any intrinsic interest in the host community but are usually willing to pay higher tuition fees. It is tempting for universities to make the security of their funding base the foremost management priority followed by reducing their reliance on government funding. Other activities, often associated with societal engagement, have a much lower priority because they do not produce a steady or sustainable income stream. Consequently, engagement is often relegated to the periphery of a university's remit with a commensurate level of funding.

All universities risk their engagement efforts giving way to what the American educationalist Dan Butin refers to as a 'distressing cultural voyeurism' if they see the local community as a laboratory where research experiments are conducted.[5] John Saltmarsh notes the range of activities that are called 'engagement' but suggests there are, or ought to be, common elements and a normative dimension.

Engagement defined by process and purpose has a particular meaning in higher education and is associated with implications for institutional change. The processes of engagement refer to the way in which those at a higher education institution – administrators, academics, staff and students – relate to those outside the higher education institution. Purpose refers specifically to enhancing a public culture of democracy on and off campus and alleviating public problems through democratic means. Processes and purposes are inextricably linked; the means must be consistent with the ends and the ends are defined by democratic culture. The norms of which are determined by the values of inclusiveness, participation, task sharing, lay participation, reciprocity in public problem solving, and an equality of respect for the knowledge and experience that everyone contributes to education and community building. Democratic processes and purpose reorient engagement to what we are calling 'democratic engagement.[6]

The champions of the civic university advocate formalising relationships with external stakeholders and establishing guidelines and expectations so that engagement is not an *ad hoc* activity that lacks an ultimate goal. The absence of a considered and measured long-term outcome usually suggests the engagement is largely opportunistic and highly susceptible to self-interest. An aspiring civic university needs individual leaders who can deconstruct the obstacles to more effective engagement and metrics to ensure investment is effective and efficient. The creation of long-standing partnerships focussed on a common vision of the future and a shared commitment to resolve intractable problems are the means by which engagement is transformed from an activity undertaken by interested individuals to a program of concerted action that embodies the institution's view of its charter and the shape of its continuing mission.

The most fulsome form of engagement involves the connection of teaching and research with solving real-world practical issues, transcending the enunciation of principles to commending participation with 'end-users' who share in the identification of problems and the validation of solutions. The civic university has attempted to recast engagement from being a third pillar standing alongside education and research into the link between teaching and research, and the means by which the relevance of both activities to the public good is assured. Thus, the definitions of teaching and research have a service element that is central and critical with a flow of information and insights from the community to the academy. The university's aim is holistic involvement in the local community and a sense in which the faculty are partners in its evolution and development rather than merely being a source of employment and commercial activity. The engagement agenda, according to James Duderstadt, 'consists of those activities that are aimed at aimed at serving the needs of society as dictated by an agenda set by the public and its representatives, rather than the institution itself'.[7]

The difficulty associated with Duderstadt's contention is in the university having confidence in the ability of the public to enunciate a coherent agenda and the absence of the university's own insights into what it can and cannot reasonably contribute given its resources and expertise. Who has authority to speak for the community? What informs their sense of the public good? And how does the University respond to criticism of its priorities from among advocacy groups who want a different ordering of priorities or entirely different objectives? If the university sponsors engagement activities, how does it avoid alienating those sectors of society who feel ignored or marginalised when their needs do not feature in an engagement plan? Should local problems have precedence over global challenges when resources make it difficult for the university to invest adequately in both over the longer term?

The same tension exists for 'challenge driven' universities, such as Arizona State University, an international partner of the University of New South Wales (UNSW). Which challenges are the most urgent: those that assist the largest number of people or those that help those in greatest need? In sum, what consultative processes will shape the university's engagement programs? Can the university remain politically neutral when many of the problems it might address and many of the solutions it might propose have political dimensions implying support or opposition to party platforms? Will emphasis be on the public interest, the public good or public value? And who gets to decide? Will the university ultimately decide because its resources are being invested or will stakeholders (who are not subject to statutory responsibilities with respect to governance) be entitled to determine where effort is directed?

Those who are not drawn to the civic university model express concern that its foundational philosophy detracts from the academic mission of the university in that it risks turning higher education institutions into service providers and organisational consultants for local government and other state instrumentalities. While the concerns are valid in principle, when it comes to practice the pressure will always be in the direction of separation and isolation from society. Yet, questions of quality remain. Chris Brink believes that the

> biggest challenge for proponents of the idea of a civic university is to give a definition or a test of quality. There is a reasonable national consensus on how to judge the quality of research and, to a lesser extent, the quality of teaching. There is still a lack of a common notion of quality of engagement. There is a danger of creating unrealistic expectations for stakeholders with and outside a higher education provider and confusing civic engagement with corporate social responsibility.[8]

This danger seems to unnerve some academic administrators who are content with the focus remaining closely on teaching and research, activities that are designed, in part, to produce academic faculty equipped to ensure the university's longevity.

Public interest and Australia's universities

There is little consistency in the engagement philosophies undergirding the activities of Australian universities. The common element seems to be widening the scope of 'external stakeholder' relationships. These stakeholders usually include government agencies, listed companies and private firms and with relationships taking the form of fee-for-service arrangements. Some of these arrangements may nominate the public interest as their principal objective. Conversely, when the public interest is defined in terms of minimising financial outlays, success in higher education is defined as either the ability to deliver more services for the same level of funding or attracting alternative sources of funding for existing services. These narrow conceptions of the public interest exclude the many other activities that universities have traditionally undertaken in the public interest and have the capacity to undertake in the future.

Among Australian universities, UNSW, known as the New South Wales University of Technology until October 1958, ought to be among the most attentive to the public interest given the highly practical element in its original charter of 1949.[9] The University's founding legislation obliges it:

> (a) to provide facilities for higher specialised instruction and advanced training in the various branches of technology and science in their application to industry and commerce; and (b) to aid by research and other suitable means the advancement, development, and practical application of science to industry and commerce.[10]

Notably, the legislation did not commit the University to defining or defending, promoting or protecting the public interest. The objects related to means and not ends. The University would contribute to professional practice (reflected in the provision of training) and would conduct research that would enhance productivity and aid economic growth. There is a presumption that these objects serve the public interest in an indirect way since the point and purpose of assisting science and technology, and advancing industry and commerce are not disclosed. There is no mention of social advancement or personal fulfilment. The absence of such a prescription was consistent with legislative drafting customs and conventions in the 1940s. It also reflected community consensus that science and technology were common goods that would generate social capital. But an editorial in the *Sydney Morning Herald* on 25 February 1950 wondered whether the UNSW charter was so narrow as to make the new institution unworthy of being called a university.

With the creation of Arts and Medical faculties in 1958, the Act was amended to change the University's name and to extend its objects to include 'the provision of instruction and carrying out of research in the disciplines of the humane studies and medicine and in such other disciplines as the Council may from time to time determine'. The 1958 amendments simply broadened the University's education and research remit. There was no attempt to say why or how the humanities and medicine advanced the public interest. The expansion of the faculties fulfilled the then Vice-Chancellor's desire for UNSW to become a general university that would enlarge the intellectual horizons of all students. As the focus remained firmly on vocational training and professional development, the public interest was presumably self-evident to the Government and to the University's executive staff. The decision to further expand its remit was delegated to the University Council, granting the University authority to determine the number and nature of faculties and, by implication, its understanding of the public needs to which it would respond.

Subsequent legislative amendments only slightly updated the objects.[11] The Act (as amended in 1989) makes the University's primary objective 'the promotion, within the limits of the University's resources, of scholarship, research, free inquiry, the interaction of research and training, and academic excellence'. A principal function, also prescribed in the Act, is 'the provision of courses of study or instruction across a range of fields, and the carrying out of research, to *meet the needs of the community* (emphasis added)'.[12] It is followed by 'participation in public discourse'. These amendments expanded the objects and drew attention to a 'primary' objective expressed in different terms to those featured in previous versions of the legislation. Although there was no attempt to links means to ends, the promotion of scholarship, free inquiry and academic excellence arguably required more of a 'public interest' explanation than the previous amendments because of the greater effective distance between the practice of scholarship, inquiry and excellence and whatever they might deliver in terms of the public interest. The assertion that the very existence of scholarship, inquiry and excellence is in the public interest might not be self-evident to those beyond the University and might require explanation. In sum, neither the original objects nor their current wording prescribe an obligation to recognise the public interest or stipulate measures for meeting the needs of the community – however these are interpreted.[13] Therefore, the University is not held to a public interest test for much of its collective activity in any formal way. It is essentially a self-imposed commitment that does not require external validation.

There may, however, be a two-fold objection to the notion that the University exists to serve the public interest. The first is that the University was established to stand apart from the body politic to challenge question-able definitions of the public interest and to chastise those whose fail in their formal responsibility to defend the public interest. Second, the University occupies a privileged position in society because in asserting its political independence and institutional autonomy it is not a government agency or state instrumentality obliged to serve the public interest regardless of how the public interest might be defined. Conversely, there is a strong public interest argument that the University and its faculty be held accountable to the same standards of collective decision-making and corporate conduct as every entity established by parliament and every person paid from the public purse. In essence, what happens at the University is of interest to the public who are entitled to ask questions about its affairs and the activities of its staff. UNSW is a publicly funded, not-for-profit entity whose staff are considered 'public officers' under state legislation such as the *Independent Commission Against Corruption Act*. Although it secures funding through competitive research grants, industry partnerships, commercialised research and philanthropy, in 2018 the University received $934 million (out of a total revenue of $1.9 billion) from government. This funding provides for academic and professional staffing activities across nine academic faculties and approximately 125 centres and institutes.[14] As the recipient of substantial public funding, UNSW is accountable to a range of stakeholders including the Commonwealth and the New South Wales State Governments who represent the Australian public and New South Wales' taxpayers. Its faculty and administrators are also personally responsible for the expenditure of substantial amounts of treasury money.

Although less reliant on public funding than a decade ago, the University continues to receive nearly half of its revenue from the public purse. By implication, and in common with every other publicly funded institution, the University is accountable to government for the use of public monies and responsible to the representatives of those who fund its activities. Consequently, it can be argued, the University's teaching, research and engagement need to be mindful of the public interest and, when and where possible, be committed to promoting the public interest to the extent that its assets allow. But other than in the responsible use of resources, ensuring that its people and programs have not been captured by political ideology, commercial interests or personal ambitions that serve an unrepresentative section of society, can the University be *required* to base its activities on the public interest when these interests are often left undefined or are difficult to determine? This is unless, of course, these interests are prescribed by parliamentarians as representatives of the people. The answer is probably 'no'. The University cannot be compelled to organise its teaching and order its research by an external authority irrespective of how persuasive a case might be for a particular engagement agenda. Nevertheless, over the past two decades, senior executives at UNSW have highlighted the University's desire to enrich Australian society, that is, to serve the public interest, through both teaching and research.

Reflecting on the University's fiftieth anniversary in 1999, former Chancellor and then Governor of New South Wales, Gordon Samuels, observed that 'since its foundation UNSW has been a leading player in the redefining of traditional notions of university life and character in Australia, maintaining its contribution to *public life* and its continuing focus on the incorporation of change' (emphasis added). By its seventieth anniversary in 2019, the University had embraced 'Strategy 2025' which features social engagement and global impact alongside excellence in teaching and research as its key objectives.[15] The Vice-Chancellor, Professor Ian Jacobs, explains that the Strategy

> sets out the overarching strategic priorities and themes which will guide us in its implementation. It outlines an innovative, ambitious and altruistic agenda, reflecting a conviction across our University community that UNSW has the potential to achieve great things during the next decade.

Further:

[o]ur aspiration for the next decade is to establish UNSW as Australia's global university. We aspire to this in the belief that a great university, which is a global leader in discovery, innovation, impact, education and thought leadership, can make an enormous difference to the lives of people in Australia and around the world. We recognise that others are not standing still and that many universities worldwide share at least some of our ambitions.[16]

There are several significant statements of intent in this preamble presuming a knowledge of, and a commitment to, the public interest. The most striking is the desire to 'make an enormous difference to the lives of people in Australia and around the world'. The University plainly sees itself as a servant of the public interest and a stakeholder in the common good. Further, its first and best energies will be directed towards the advancement of human civilisation. Its efforts are not accidental or coincidental. The University seeks to make an 'enormous difference' through its leadership in discovery, innovation, impact, education and thought leadership. There is an implied cause and effect relationship but the application of leadership – and the exercise of thought leadership – ensures that the desire to 'make an enormous difference to the lives of people in Australia and around the world' is an objective rather than a mere aspiration that can be left to chance.

Notwithstanding its laudable intent, a number of fundamental questions need to be asked of this expansive vision statement. What kind of difference is the University seeking to make? How does and will the University decide where the need it seeks to address is greatest or most pressing? Will the senior leadership group make judgements about the public interest and areas of priority teaching and research or should the discretion to make decisions of this kind reside with individual academics? Should UNSW look to external stakeholders for help in identifying or clarifying the public interest and seek a consensus on the engagement agenda to which the University might respond? As the efficiency and effectiveness of Australian universities face increased public scrutiny, UNSW is under mounting pressure to demonstrate how the University, as a recipient of substantial amounts of public money, serves the public interest. Imposing a public interest test on the University's activities prompts some problematic questions but none are insurmountable. They require consultation and the building of consensus. But as a first step in declaring its intent, the University's legislation might be amended.

Embracing the public interest

Modern universities like UNSW are vast corporate entities with complex internal constituencies and large diverse clientele. Their charters include the delivery of courses at the undergraduate and postgraduate levels, the conduct of research with a focus on pure and applied knowledge, and engagement with the host society by offering its expertise and experience for the betterment of humanity. Given the objects to which universities must direct their energies are unclear and noting the expansive vision that propels its Strategy 2025, the UNSW Act could simply be amended with the replacement of the words 'to meet the needs of the community' with 'to serve the public interest' (Part 2, Section 6, UNSW Act). The public interest is usually larger than community need with a remit that would reasonably extend beyond the eastern suburbs of Sydney – the community in which UNSW is physically located.

To give this commitment a coherent form and some urgency, the University might consider producing a stand-alone annual public interest report each year highlighting the alignment of its programs and priorities with the public interest – however it is defined or depicted – which would give a sharper edge and a clearer focus to all engagement activities. The proposed legislative amendment is, of course, largely symbolic although inclusion of 'the public interest' would align the University with most other bodies that have been created by an act of the New South Wales Parliament, that is, to always act in the public interest.

My proposal does not entail a major shift of mindset or a radical recasting of the University's operations. UNSW has exuded elements of the emerging 'civic university' model since its establishment. In terms of the three distinct strands of engagement, UNSW has displayed elements of each because it has not embraced either a comprehensive or a unitary approach to its 'external relations'. In many respects, it is a hybrid university that retains the original emphasis on science, engineering and technology with emerging strengths in law and public policy. But there would be merit in the University identifying its preferred model for engagement – my own clear preference is for the public good strand – and allowing discussion of the possibilities and problems of the alternatives to sharpen existing statements of intent which are inconsistent and possibly incompatible. Moreover, without a declared commitment to the public interest, the University risks pursuing agendas and making investments that do not represent the best use of taxpayer's money and which might, if only inadvertently, advance private or sectional interests to the detriment of the whole society. If nothing else, attentiveness to the public interest would serve as an effective and efficient operating premise that ensured community goodwill and political support.

Endnotes

1   www.upp-foundation.org/publications/foundation-glyn-davis-lecture-report, delivered at the Globe Theatre, London on 19 October 2017.
2   theconversation.com/the-modern-university-must-reinvent-itself-to-survive-37, 11 March 2011.
3   John Goddard, Ellen Hazelkorn, Louise Kempton and Paul Vallance (eds), *The Civic University: the Policy and Leadership Challenges*, Edward Elgar Publishing, Cheltenham, 2016, p. x.
4   Jussi Valimaa, 'University revolutions and academic capitalism: a historical perspective' in Brendan Cantwell and Ilkka Kauppinen (eds), *Academic Capitalism in the Age of Globalisation*, Johns Hopkins University Press, Baltimore, 2014, p. 46.
5   Dan Butin, 'When engagement is not enough: building the next generation of the engaged campus', in Dan Butin and Scott Seider (eds), *The Engaged Campus: Certificates, Minors and Majors as the New Community Engagement*, Palgrave Macmillan, New York, 2012, p. 5.
6   John Saltmarsh, Matthew Hartley and Patti Clayton, Democratic Engagement – White Paper, New England Resource Centre for Higher Education, University of Massachusetts, Boston, 2009, https://repository.upenn.edu/gse_pubs/274/.
7   James Duderstadt, *A University for the 21st Century*, University of Michigan Press, Ann Arbor, 2000, p. 133.
8   Chris Brink and John Hogan, 'Newcastle University and the development of the concept of a world-class civic university', in Goddard et al (eds), *The Civic University*, p. 253.
9   See Patrick O'Farrell's *UNSW: A Portrait*, UNSW Press, 1999. UNSW was originally established as the New South Wales University of Technology under the *Technical Education and New South Wales University of Technology Act, 1949*. On 7 October 1958, ascent was given by the Governor of New South Wales to Act No. 24, 1958, of the New South Wales Parliament amending the principal Act under which the

University operates. This amendment provided for the renaming of the entity to the 'University of New South Wales'. The seventieth anniversary of the founding of UNSW will be marked on 1 July 2019. At its inception, UNSW was the second university to be established in the State, and the eighth university to be operating in Australia.

10 https://www.legislation.nsw.gov.au/acts/1949-11.pdf.

11 https://www.legislation.nsw.gov.au/#/view/act/1989/125.

12 https://www.legislation.nsw.gov.au/#/view/act/1989/125/sch2a.

13 In New South Wales there are over 190 pieces of legislation requiring the public interest to be considered when implementing an Act of Parliament or in making particular administrative decisions under the Act. The legislation includes the *Defamation Act 2005, Evidence Act 1995, Environmental Planning and Assessment Act 1979, Government Information (Public Access) Act 2009, Local Government Act 1993, Ombudsman Act 1974, Police Act 1990, Privacy and Personal Information Protection Act 1998, Public Interest Disclosures Act 1994, Public Sector Employment and Management Act 2002, and Teaching Service Act 1980.* The UNSW Act (1989) does not prescribe a public interest test. .

14 UNSW Financial Report 2016, p. 12; Australian Government funding of universities is currently $17 billion per annum (figure provided in speech delivered by the Minister for Education, Senator Simon Birmingham, 28 February 2018).

15 See *UNSW 2025 Strategy, Our Strategic Priorities and Themes* released in October 2015 https://www.2025.unsw.edu.au/sites/default/files/uploads/unsw_2025strategy_201015.pdf .

16 UNSW 2025 Strategy, p.4.

POSTSCRIPT

Tom Frame

Most contemporary accounts of the public interest are highly dependent on context or circumstances to give them coherence. According to some practitioners it is difficult, if not impossible, to decide whether the public interest has been promoted or protected without reference to a specific objective being served or a particular principle being advanced by either a policy or a process. A government policy is said to promote the public interest when, for instance, social cohesion is increased in tangible ways or community wellbeing is enhanced in some demonstrable sense. And yet, neither the context nor the circumstance actually defines the public interest. Their function is essentially to confirm and then illustrate that a policy or a process serves more than private individuals and their personal ambitions. There are implicit conceptual assertions in all accounts of the public interest purporting to reply on context and circumstance for their consistency and conviction.

Unchallenged assertions and unexamined assumptions

Given the political significance and practical seriousness that is associated with public interest claims, it is surprising that these conceptual assertions have been largely ignored in favour of making practical determinations of what constitutes the public interest in relation to specific policies and particular processes. I recognise that policymakers and process managers need to deal with real world problems and make real time decisions about what best serves the public interest as they perceive it. But it is the unexamined aspects of this approach to the public interest that concern me most. In this book, and in the previous one in the series, there are many unchallenged and, I would suggest, questionable assumptions about both the nature of the public and character of its interests. The absence of reflection might flow from the fact that everyone is a member of the public with interests that are rarely unique. In other words, we presume to know what the public interest entails or where it might lie. That being so, we assume an understanding of the public interest that is sufficient for the purpose of either making public interest claims or critiquing the claims made by others.

But the unintended consequence of these assumptions remaining untested lies in the frequency and ease with which public interest claims are made and the lack of consensus that is soon apparent when such claims are examined closely. As the public interest is cited regularly as a characteristic of good policy and invoked repeatedly as a feature of sound decision-making in the hope of finding consensus in a dis-integrating body politic, there is growing suspicion of deception and duplicity. As a principle without peer in public administration, there is real danger that the misuse and abuse of the public interest as a defining concept will see open societies undergirded by participatory democracy losing something valuable that cannot be readily replaced. If public interest criteria or public interest tests were to fall into disrepute or disuse, it is difficult to know what would take their place. The common good is not synonymous with the public interest nor is the notion of social capital. They each consist of different things and play a different role in personal relations and political interactions. Hence, my continuing interest in trying to determine what we mean (or ought to mean) by the public interest *before* it is applied to practical problems and concrete circumstances.

There are two general objections to my objective. First, if a nuanced concept of the public interest were developed, would it have any practical value? I believe it would, as I hope to show. Second, might there be benefit in leaving the public interest undefined if the lack of conceptual clarity prompts discussion of practical matters that bear upon whether a claimed public interest really exists and can be measured? The purported benefits of this line of thinking are uncertain. Most uses of the public interest relying on context and circumstance involve an element of concession and compromise. Concessions are frequently offered to special needs and advocacy groups on the grounds of fairness or equity while compromises are extended to those unintentionally harmed or hindered by a policy or a process. For instance, a government decides to increase subsidies to farmers and allowances to carers because it wants to address perceived inequity or hardship. It does these things, in part, to fulfil an ideological agenda and attract electoral recognition. These subsidies and the allowances might not survive a public interest test but the government proceeds regardless because it wants, among other things, to secure the support of farmers and to avoid the ire of carers. Alternatively, a financial regulator decides against prosecuting a well-known and popular sporting figure because it fears press criticism of its past oversight and allegations of persecution but resolves to pursue a high-profile but unpopular business executive to convey a general message about its future intentions which it presumes the community will welcome.

When these things happen, and they often happen when a matter has some cultural sensitivity or electoral benefit, the public interest can rapidly mutate into a partisan position that reflects the preferences and the prejudices of particular individuals and groups irrespective of whether they are elected or appointed. Those making concessions and offering compromises are no longer primarily pursuing the public interest but an ideological outcome or an administrative settlement. They are essentially controlling stakeholders and managing expectations rather than focussing on whatever serves the undifferentiated public and its interests. This is an observation not a criticism. Legislation and administration are complex and complicated activities. My point is that the public interest has been subordinated to other considerations. Self-interest, however dispersed it might seem, has been pursued ahead of the public interest. Rather than focussing on the tangible outcomes of a policy or a process, a better approach to ensuring a more reliable account to the public interest is to focus on the individual citizen and the duties of citizenship.

Citizenship and the transcendence of self

In the modern world, birthplace is the most common source of citizenship. Other than those who acquire citizenship from their parents or who seek citizenship in another country either through marriage or prolonged residency, where we are born will usually determine where we will live most of our lives. Further, we recognise nationality forms part of our personal identity. That being so, we generally accept a sense of obligation for our nation and promote its standing in the world, if only to the extent of defending its reputation from detractors. In addition to state or regional loyalties, which come with their own responsibilities as well as rights, there are cultural ties and familial bonds which also impose obligations. These responsibilities and obligations are the origins of our sense of the public interest.

From infancy, human beings are taught to consider the needs and wants of others, beginning with those of family and friends extending to known and then to unknown others to whom more than mere acknowledgement is expected. Within families the individual is neither supreme nor absolute. Children learn that they can and sometimes must rely on others and their goodwill to survive and to thrive. Adults are drawn to people from whom they can seek assistance and with whom life's burdens can be shared. It is the interactions between human beings that make it possible for individuals to discern their identity and glean their destiny. While philosophers might assert the primacy of the individual in societies where government curtails individual liberties and restricts individual freedoms, they also accept that individuals are drawn almost inexorably into communities and find contentment in their relationships – filial, social and political. As community life contributes much to an individual's enjoyment of life, community-mindedness and public spiritedness are encouraged for their own sake and for what they deliver.

The *Oxford Dictionary* defines community-mindedness as being 'interested in helping the wider community'. A slight variation is public-spiritedness which is being motivated by a commitment to public welfare. The first is generally propelled by altruism and the second by duty. Those who are community-minded will bring families and neighbourhoods together in pursuit of common goals with shared outcomes in the hope of enriching them. People who are public-spirited will contribute to programs and projects that enhance the places where individuals gather and from which they find fulfilment. In both instances, there is transcendence of ego and self either for altruistic reasons – a heartfelt desire to see others flourish – or from pursuit of existential meaning beyond individual satisfaction – there is nobility in serving others. To a large degree, public interest claims originate with individual values and personal virtues. These values and virtues are the lens through which a person views themselves, regards their neighbour and imagines the world. A community-minded person will look beyond themselves and even their kindred group as a function of deeply held beliefs about the character and composition of humankind. A public-spirited person will focus on the interactions between people in community life based on their convictions about the realisation of human potential. These sentiments are about more than simply putting others before oneself. They involve a vision of human society within which human being is expressed and individual fulfilment is found.

The modern nation-state has co-opted a narrative drawn from this vision that has been useful in promoting the nation – which purports to be greater than the sum of its individual citizens – and the state – the vehicle by which collective value is generated – as institutions that are intended to serve the public interest. The legitimacy of the nation-state is built on a covenant between the leaders and the led that is based on consent, conveyed through free and fair elections. It is sustained by trust in the honesty of those holding public office and in the integrity of public institutions. Individual citizens are not entitled to abrogate their citizenship and its obligations, if only the duty to obey the law of the land, unless they relocate and reside elsewhere. [Even then, their citizenship might persist in the eyes of the nation-state that originally granted it.] Citizenship is a powerful cultural and political force with enormous capacity to inspire and energise an otherwise disparate community of people. It is usually considered a prized possession and a special privilege when imbued with patriotism and nationalism.

State tyranny and the common good

The vision of collaborating citizens forming a cooperative society to pursue common interests is not free from challenge. Indeed, nearly 400 years ago the political philosopher, Thomas Hobbes, feared the evolving nation-state (the proto-type of most Western democracies) was a poor replacement for the absolutist monarchy that had been overthrown by the British in 1648. In his treatise *Leviathan* which was published in 1651 following the proclamation of a Commonwealth after the execution of King Charles I, Hobbes advanced another view of society. He stressed the right of the individual to determine the course of his or her own life free from interference.[1] Because these interests – which are paramount - occasionally converge or collide, he conceded that individuals must surrender some of their liberty and discretion to a supreme authority – the great Leviathan of the 'state' – which possessed the authority and wielded the power necessary to ensure that competing goals or conflicting ambitions were harmonized or, at least, reconciled. This was a minimalist view of the public interest, reflecting the times in which he was writing. After a bitter civil war that had raged for six years, Hobbes' priority was reducing conflict rather than increasing cooperation.

In Hobbes' worldview, there is no attempt to identify what is good or bad nor to encourage virtue and discourage vice. What we call good or virtuous, according to Hobbes, is little more than preference or prejudice. Rationality, which is crucial to this outlook, is understood as a conscious promoting of what promotes one's interests and deliberate avoidance of what doesn't. The philosophers John Rawls in *A Theory of Justice*[2] and Robert Nozick in *Anarchy, State and Utopia*[3] have reclothed the vision of Hobbes in modern attire. The story they tell is of humanity as an aggregate of rational self-seeking individuals. They see society as an arena of contrasting and competing interests in which the resolution of conflict is the work of centralised authority given legitimacy by a social contract but only to the extent that it maximizes the self-interest of the individual participants.

An alternate view, and the one that undergirds much contemporary thinking about the public interest, draws on religious convictions about the nature of humanity and the character of human society. The Hebrew Bible, known throughout the Christian world as the 'Old Testament', offers a fulsome account of humanity's origins and destiny beginning with the opening narrative of Genesis: 'In the beginning, God created ... and it was good'. The universe unfolds according to a plan in which humanity finds meaning conveyed through two linked propositions. The first affirms the sanctity of the human individual *as individual*. Every person is uniquely created in the 'image of God'. But the second proposition asserts the incompleteness of the individual *as individual*: 'It is not good to be alone'. Hence, the need for relationships and for stable structures within which these formative and definitive relationships can be sustained. In the Biblical view, the individual is, therefore, to be understood in relation to others and, hence, to derive identity from them: 'I am my father's son ... I am my teacher's student'. These relationships expand from the nuclear to the extended family, and are then manifested in the clan, the tribe and ultimately the nation. And they are enclosed by a covenant: a statement of privileges and obligations that embodies a sense of identity and basis of dignity. Covenants are maintained by the relationships of those bound by them. They primarily express the kind of persons the covenanted people are to be.

The former Chief Rabbi of the United Kingdom, Jonathan Sacks, high-lighted the crucial distinction between the story offered in Hobbes' *Leviathan* and the one presented in Genesis.[4] It is the central figure. For Hobbes it is 'I', over and against everyone else. In the Bible it is the 'we' of which I am a part, meaning marriage, the family, the clan and the nation. In this account, individual affiliations, associations and attachments are not irrelevant, but essential, to the structure of obligations human beings form and the manner in which they are held accountable. Individuals owe duties to others because they are part of an individual's identity. The driving force in this vision of society is not maximised self-interest but a series of covenantal obligations that include the duties and responsibilities that flow from identification and belonging. Whereas the parties to a contract can disengage when it is no longer to their benefit to continue, a covenant is more binding because it is built on fidelity and loyalty. Covenental language is, therefore, better suited to talking about the public interest than that of the contract although declining familiarity with biblical precepts and religious doctrines in the post-Christian period means this language is less well-known and less widely-appreciated.

Individuals and the public interest

In contemporary Australia, there is tension between the story originally told by Hobbes and the account of human origins and destiny in Genesis. Individualism, the belief that the individual alone and unaided is both capable and entitled to determine what is good or bad, true or false, is a prevailing mindset among a segment of the population. For those of this view, the location of meaning and purpose is found in individual self-fulfilment, some-thing that will inevitably vary among and between people. It is also evident that the common life of most Australians is sustained by a number of social, political and economic contracts that presume or embody some sense of the public interest. It cannot be otherwise for stable, orderly and productive interactions between people to be sustained. Perhaps more important than contracts in terms of human fulfillment is the need for covenants and the values and virtues undergirding and fulfilling them.

My account of the public interest begins with values and virtues more than rights and entitlements in order to preserve and protect the covenants that allow meaning-imparting and identity-giving relationships to be maintained and to mature. A well-developed appreciation of the public interest begins with a commitment to developing the collective character of the public whose interests are being promoted. Laws promoting selfless attitudes and denouncing selfish actions are not the answer in a free society. The identification of values and the inculcation of virtues is not something at which states excel. An accurate and well-articulated sense of the public interest is built on the covenants that emerge from moral communities who are able to teach values and to train their members in the acquisition of virtues. I have argued elsewhere that I believe the Australian Public Service, for instance, is 'thick' enough to operate as a moral community. Indeed, it has no alternative but to act as a moral community given what its people need to be, in doing what they exist to do.

If there is no sense of individuals being part of a particular kind of community with membership that infers certain mutual obligations and leadership that exists principally to promote the common good, if there is resistance to accountability within and beyond the community, such a group of people will face either internal incoherence and implode or suffer external interference and explode. The orientation of individual free-will, which is at the heart of this matter, is decisive. If an individual believes they have primacy and then thinks and acts that everything and everyone revolves around them, that their interests are always and everywhere to be pursued ahead of those of the community, the inevitable outcomes will include the absence of empathy and a lack of compassion. It is possible for a society to erect barriers, hurdles and fences to restrain, frustrate and curtail self-interest exercised without regard to its broader consequences. Self-interest will, however, eventually succeed if it persists as the main focus of individual first and best efforts.

The continuing struggle between the individual and the community is the starting point for an account of the public interest. For the public interest to prevail as a standard by which policies and processes are developed, there needs to be thorough and continuing attention to shifting the focus from 'we' rather than 'I' but, at the same time, giving due regard to the entitlement of individuals to pursue their personal goals and private aspirations without hindrance or interference. This is an administrative, philosophical, ethical and political challenge. When I know who I am as a person, and what I am to be within my community, identifying or locating the public interest becomes a less vexing question.

Individuals are more likely to flourish in a society that esteems commitment and cooperation, generosity and compassion, because common wealth – an aspirational term that was used to denote the kind of society that those who worked towards Australian Federation in 1901 hoped to create – is expanded and and thereby made more accessible and more available for re-investment in individual endeavour. There is a corollary in the United States and the hopes of John Adams, Thomas Jefferson, Benjamin Franklin and James Madison who thought the attitude of the citizenry to national life was critical to the health and welfare of the American republic.[5] Notably, private organisations and public companies are also expected to demonstrate social responsibility. A mindset founded on the conviction that individuals can achieve more and find greater fulfilment working together and collaboratively than striving alone and unaided is the unspoken basis for most accounts of the public interest.

Citizenship and public interest convictions

In his seminal essay, 'The Public Interest', published in 1964, Brian Barry was concerned principally with interests.[6] In arguing that intention was the crucial element in public interest claims, Barry draws on Jean-Jacques Rousseau's *Social Contract* and his discussion of the 'general will' and the 'less general will' of the people. Rousseau's faith in widespread civic virtue, which is consistent with a positive attitude to the duties of citizenship, leads to the right question being asked: 'what measure [meaning policy] will benefit me in common with everyone else, rather than me at the expense of everyone else?'[7] According to Rousseau, in a well-ordered state 'the aggregate of the common happiness furnishes a greater proportion of that of each individual'. The individual does not consider his or her own interests apart from community interests. The two are linked if not interwoven. Thus, Barry notes, disagreements about the public interest are 'due only to conflicts of opinion – not to conflicts of interest'. I agree with both Rousseau and Barry but with one important qualification: there is greater likelihood of consensus on the public interest when the individual thinks and acts as a *citizen*. It is a matter of mindset.

I am drawing attention to what I believe is a crucial distinction between the individual as a citizen, the individual as a voter who elects candidates to public office and the individual as a private person with the freedom to live his or her life as they choose. This distinction matters because citizens have obligations that transcend those of voters and private persons. Voters are entitled, if not encouraged, to place the interests of the local community ahead of national interests; private persons have the liberty to pursue whatever they think are their best interests. The citizen is, however, expected to put aside ideological commitments and personal preferences in considering the interests of the state or the nation and what serves its wellbeing. It is possible, of course, for the interests of the voter and the private person to overlap or coincide. These interests do not necessarily diverge. But in making determinations about where the public interest might lie and in making decisions about what constitutes the public interest, the individual acting as citizen rather than as voter or private person is better placed and more positively disposed to protecting or promoting interests that might conflict or stand apart from their interests as a voter or a private person. Barry also notes that 'interests which are shared by few can be promoted by them whereas interests shared by many have to be furthered by the state if they are to be furthered at all.'[8]

The purpose of government is developing policies and devising processes that promote or protect the public interest – once it has been identified. My principal claim in this postscript is to note that this identification requires an informed citizenry whose character is animated by the civic virtues that flow from an education system that inculcates the knowledge and skills that are needed for participation in political and social life. In other words, it requires men and women to act as citizens who set aside their personal and private interests and arbitrate on what best serves the entire community. In discerning the public interest, they are no longer people whose judgement relies on personal considerations for their shape and substance.

The public interest: an alternate start point

My account of the public interest is different in placing greater weight on the actual discernment of interests than on descriptions of the public and emphasising the place and function of citizenship in determinations of where the public interest might lie. We do not need to quibble over descriptions or depictions of the public when the focus is the common life of the citizenry. Discerning the public interest is not the task of some but the work of many. I am conscious of the need to develop this line of thinking further and to deal with a range of reasonable objections. My aim here is to suggest another approach which I think has merit, especially given the frequency and forcefulness with which public interest claims are made. This approach has the potential to counter the partisanship and the special pleading that is implicit in so many contemporary assertions of the public interest. There needs to be closer attention to the character of public interest claimants and the capacities – personal and professional – that are operative when they deal with any public interest consideration.

The American political philosopher Ralph Ketcham has argued in *Public-Spirited Citizenship* that the place of the public interest in political life has been undermined by those academic disciplines that highlighted differences between individuals and distinctions in culture which made the idea (or perhaps ideal) of a public interest look unscientific and naïve.[9] Public life was, representatives of these disciplines asserted, a struggle for power and the assertion of supremacy. Human nature was chaotic; human choices were unpredictable. The desire to identify the public interest was little more than an attempt to impose order and secure compliance with the preferences of the powerful than a process by which autonomous and thoughtful individuals discerned the things that enriched human living. Ketcham believes suspicion of the public interest as a tool of political control or a weapon of partisan rhetoric is greatly exaggerated. They reflect a lack of faith in education and its ability to impart moral virtue. I share his conclusions.

For the public interest to be rescued from its current misuse and overuse, those who invoke or claim the public interest need to be conscious of, and show respect for, the character of the concept they are handling. The citizen has the foremost claim to authority in asserting that something is in the public interest. Political operatives, media commentators and community leaders are entitled, and should be encouraged, to engage in discussions and even debates about the public interest but they should do so as engaged *citizens*. They need to embrace the mind and the mood of the citizen and speak as people who have reflected upon, and then transcended, their own preferences and prejudices when they deal with any matter with a public interest status. In essence, I am isolating public interest claims from routine political discourse and contending that the participants in any discussion of the public interest first need to remember their duties as citizens. They might be treated by the community in a similar way to Federal Parliament's handling of purported 'matters of public importance'. In other words, they are dealt with in a particular way. My hope is there will be fewer public interest claims and, when such claims are made, they are more modest and mediated first through the lens of responsible citizenship.

The account of the public interest presented here is a work-in-progress. What I am prescribing might seem artificial and impractical. I accept this objection but do not accept that it constitutes a fatal flaw. These kinds of objection can be addressed and ameliorated because points of general principle are not at stake. But if this postscript were to contribute nothing more than directing attention to the standing and motivation of those making a public interest claim or fulfilling a public interest duty, I will be content with such an outcome.

Endnotes

1   Thomas Hobbes, *Leviathan or The Matter, Forme and Power of a Common-Wealth Ecclesiasticall and Civil*, for an annotated copy see https://earlymoderntexts.com/assets/pdfs/hobbes1651part1.pdf.
2   John Rawls, *A Theory of Justice*, Harvard University Press, Harvard, 1971.
3   Robert Nozick, *Anarchy, State and Utopia*, Basic Books, New York, 1974.
4   See Jonathan Sachs, *The Politics of Hope*, Jonathan Cape, London, 1997.
5   For a discussion of the relationship between private self-interest and public-spirited action see Ralph Ketcham, *Public-Spirited Citizenship: Leadership and Good Government in the United States*, Taylor & Francis, Somerset, 2015.
6   BM Barry, 'The Public Interest', *Proceedings of the Aristotelian Society, Supplementary Volumes*, vol. 38, 1964, pp. 1–38, p. 5 quoted.
7   Barry, 'The Public Interest', p. 11.
8   Barry, 'The Public Interest', p. 16.
9   Ralph Ketcham, *Public-Spirited Citizenship: leadership and good government in the United States*, Transaction, Piscataway, New Jersey, 2015.

www.ingramcontent.com/pod-product-compliance
Lightning Source LLC
Chambersburg PA
CBHW061249220326
41599CB00028B/5592